MW01223550

Oh My God!

*memories of growing up
in "the land down under"*

Wendy McGregor

Dear Lloyd
I hope you get just as
much enjoyment out of
reading this as I did in
writing it 😊

Enjoy
Wendy

Nov 23-04

TRAFFORD
on-demand publishing service™

Note for Librarians: a cataloguing record for this book that includes Dewey Decimal
Classification and US Library of Congress numbers is available from the Library and
Archives of Canada. The complete cataloguing record can be obtained from their online
database at:
www.collectionscanada.ca/amicus/index-e.html
ISBN 1-4120-3893-6
Printed in Victoria, BC, Canada

All photographs copyright © Wendy McGregor
Email address: wkmcg@telus.net

Cartoon illustrations throughout this book created and
copyright © by Raymond Rodriguez.
Email address: rayjet38@pacificcoast.net

Photograph restoration by John Joinson
Email address: jaypjay@telus.net

Cover/Book design and electronic page layout by
Image Hunter / Roy Williams
Email address: r_williams@shaw.ca

TRAFFORD

Offices in Canada, USA, Ireland, UK and Spain
This book was published *on-demand* in cooperation with Trafford Publishing. On-demand
publishing is a unique process and service of making a book available for retail sale to the
public taking advantage of on-demand manufacturing and Internet marketing. On-demand
publishing includes promotions, retail sales, manufacturing, order fulfilment, accounting and
collecting royalties on behalf of the author.
Book sales for North America and international:
Trafford Publishing, 6E–2333 Government St.,
Victoria, BC v8t 4p4 CANADA
phone 250 383 6864 (toll-free 1 888 232 4444)
fax 250 383 6804; email to orders@trafford.com
Book sales in Europe:
Trafford Publishing (UK) Ltd., Enterprise House, Wistaston Road Business Centre,
Wistaston Road, Crewe, Cheshire CW2 7RP UNITED KINGDOM
phone 01270 251 396 (local rate 0845 230 9601)
facsimile 01270 254 983; orders.uk@trafford.com
Order online at:
www.trafford.com/robots/04-1701.html

10 9 8 7 6 5 4 3 2 1

Introduction

For many years now I've told stories about my childhood, and oftentimes someone would say, "you should write a book!". Well here it is, a memoir, as I see it, growing up in Australia. A narrative of our life, and a keepsake to hand down to our children, and our grandchildren.

We frequently ask ourselves questions about the past, but all too often it is forgotten, as if it never was, and our memories are replaced by more recent events. They are often only aroused when reminiscing with loved ones. Throughout this book you will find stories coming from my senses, the way I remember them, but my family have also contributed. For when I told them what I was doing, they were inspired and spurred on to also look into their past. After the chapter I devoted to each of them, you will find their own memories.

On recollecting past events, we often found ourselves contradicting each other, however this wasn't because of our uncertainties about the past, but rather the age of the person at the time of the event. For no matter how I see things, these thoughts coming from my senses, can be seen so differently in the eyes of someone else. So different in the eyes of a sibling much older or younger, in a family with thirteen children.

Because of the Aussie jargon and the different ways in which we spell some of our words, I have included a glossary of words in the back of the book.

My memories of our past start with our mother Thelma

(affectionately nicknamed the Colonel by her sons-in-law), followed by our father Bill, our stepfather Bob, then my siblings descending from the oldest Coral, to Shane the youngest. The account of incidents and events throughout each person's memories are in no particular order, and were written as they came to mind. However not all of my family shared their memories; not for lack of wanting to, but rather a shyness in reflecting their feelings on paper or because they had passed away.

Life was full of adventure, sadness, confusion and drama in our house, but I guess it depended on how old you were at the time, that made them adventurous, sad, confusing or dramatic events, and when I think back to our childhood years, I'm caught between pain and laughter. Pain, when I think of things I would rather forget, and laughter so great, it brings tears to my eyes.

With so many different personalities in the one household, things weren't always as they appeared, but it isn't until years later when reminiscing, that we realized just how all of our personalities intermingled and made us into the secure and determined people we are today. We each resembled our parents, but we were different in our own small, but distinct way. Myself, I'm smack bang in the middle of six boys and six girls, and although we were never well off, I often thought we were, because of our closeness. We had a lot of joy in our lives, and we were never short of love and support for each other.

The Naming of the Book

When I first started writing this journal I was on my way to Australia to see my youngest sister Carol for what I thought would be the last time, and at the time of putting pen to paper I had no idea how it would evolve. Within a few hours of my flight however and with the help of a Canadian student on her way to Australia for a school excursion, the name of the book would be decided.

A little gem, Krista had been sitting beside me for several hours, and when I finally heaved a sigh of relief, put my pen down, and closed the first 20 pages of my journal, we started talking. She asked what was so engrossing that kept me so focused for so long; especially with so many students around me making such a ruckus. I told her that I was writing about my family, and she asked if she could read it, but before giving it to her, as it was in its infancy, I apologized for the roughness and misspelling she was about to encounter.

She started reading it quietly to herself, but every now and again out of her mouth would pop the words "Oh My God, did this really happen?". She said this several times and thanks to Krista, the name of the book, "Oh My God" was decided.

Acknowledgment.

This book could not have been done without the love and support of my family, who I hope will take it in the reminiscing, lighthearted way that is was intended. Each of them had such a positive outlook on life, and their contribution to this book is immeasurable.

It is a love story, for no matter what trials and tribulations, struggles and adventures we experienced, we were always there for each other. At times with minimal resources, but with enough love and support for each other, that we could overcome the most difficult of obstacles.

To my mother Thelma, and my many brothers and sisters, Coral, Dawn, Teresa, Barton, Desley, Victor, Tony and Shane. After reading this, I hope your families have a better understanding of who you are and where you came from. To our dad Bill, and siblings Jacqueline, Billy, Gary and Carol, you will always be in our hearts.

To my friends, Patsy, Peggy and Poppy, for the many hours we have spent talking about our hopes and dreams and the motivation you have shown me throughout the process of writing this.

My dear husband, Keith for your continued support and encouragement. For helping me feel good about myself, and comforting me when the memories drowned me to the point of tears.

And to my three sons, Jason, Jeffrey and Wade, this book is for you, your children and your grandchildren; to see what it was like for your uncles, aunts and grandparents living in Australia during the forties, fifties and sixties. I love you dearly.

CHAPTER ONE

The Beginning

DECEMBER 9, 2000 AND WHAT other reason to be heading back home to Australia at this time of the year, than to celebrate Christmas with my family. Well, I wish that were the case but it's not, I'm going back to see my youngest sister Carol who is in the last stages of a cancer that has decimated her body for the past four years.

The only member of my family to live overseas, since moving to Canada in December 1992, I am forever hungry for an opportunity to catch up with them. My feelings as I boarded planes previous to this trip have always been predictable and full of excitement, but as I boarded this flight, a feeling of melancholy came over me that would engross me for the entire trip.

I started writing almost as soon as I got on the plane, and in order to get a true sense of what I was feeling, every time something came to mind I closed my eyes. The memories danced vividly as if it were yesterday with each one triggering another. I recall fond memories of my childhood experiences, with some of them disclosing others that I would rather forget. I found myself trying to push these aside to concentrate on the lighthearted happier times, but they occasionally forced their way back as if to say, "hold on there, if you think you're going to write about our family and not mention everything that happened to us, you've got another thing coming"

All of the things we did as kids came flooding back, and I saw my mother standing in front of a huge wooden stove with her apron on as she stirred the large pot of porridge for breakfast. If I had to think of one memory for each of my siblings and parents, my mother would be doing just that, with my father sitting at the kitchen table listening to the radio; egging on the bets he had placed earlier that day, with the occasional gloomy look on his face as they once again crossed the line last.

My brothers and sisters are all down at the beach running around like maniacs, throwing threepenny bungers at each other, or jumping off the gun emplacements with towels wrapped around their heads and pretending to be Superman. I found myself having to dig deeper to recall the memories of my younger and older siblings, but those around my own age took little effort.

So here I am, starting on a journey that may change my

life and those around me, whether it be good or bad I'm not sure, but I do know that right now I'm feeling passionate about what I'm doing and looking forward to what it will bring. My nieces, nephews, children and grandchildren can only benefit from what they are about to read, for it will open their eyes to our experiences in a different time and place.

CHAPTER TWO

My Memories of my Mother,
Thelma Jean Wright
(Born December 8, 1920)

I DON'T KNOW HOW SHE DID IT, raising thirteen kids, who by the way, didn't turn out too bad. We all had chores to do around the house before going to school, with some of us making the beds, while others did the dishes, floors and washing. When we came home from school, the washing had to be taken off the line and put away, the table set for dinner, and of course, homework. So really, when you think about it, the only thing Mum had to worry about was how she was going to clothe and feed us. That's all!

During the forties, fifties and sixties in Australia there wasn't such a thing as government assistance, and if Dad wasn't working it was difficult for Mum to put food on the table. During these times, she often relied on the kindness of the Catholic church, and the local shop keepers who allowed her to rack up bills until she managed to pay them off. She made meals that went a long way, and we often found ourselves eating soup for breakfast, lunch and dinner.

Many times she bought offal and the cheaper cuts of meats, and we frequently found ourselves eating things that other kids would turn their noses up at. Tripe, brains, pigs feet and tongue were all part of our staple diet, but Mum had a way of cooking these so that even the most fastidious person would not recognize them.

Well known as the lining of a cows stomach, the thought of eating tripe for some of us was repulsive. For this reason, Mum used to give fish to those who didn't like tripe, and the rest of us the tripe. She would take the raw tripe out of the fridge, and lay the leather like white pieces of blubber on the kitchen table, and proceed to prepare it for dinner. For those who didn't like tripe, she would cut it into fish fillet shapes, and coat them in batter, and for the rest of us, she prepared the traditional tripe recipe. By the time we arrived home from school she would have dinner prepared, with us none the wiser that we were all eating tripe, and she had simply cooked it two different ways. I loved tripe, and to this day I haven't found anyone who can cook it as well as Mum did.

Along with the brains came the stories of who they belonged to, and I'm sure the younger ones really did believe they were human; English or Aussie I'm not sure, as we were told that both were hard to find. She would boil the brains for 20 to 30 minutes and after letting them cool, she would cut them up, coat them in flour, egg and breadcrumbs, and fry them in a little oil. By the time she finished cooking them, they looked like little golden nuggets and tasted great.

With the pigs feet Mum made the best pea and ham soup, and this along with a slice of bread to break into it, was often enough to fill us up. The aroma that filled the house while she was cooking it made your mouth water, and she only had to call us once to get us all to the table.

Tongue was one of my favorites, and to make sure she had enough, Mum would always buy the biggest one. It was huge, and I couldn't believe that there was an animal around big enough to fit this thing in its mouth, and still manage to breathe. She would press the tongue into a round steaming pot and boil it for hours, but after it cooled, and she turned it out, it bore no resemblance to the long grotesque thing she had started with. She would thinly slice it, and make the best tongue and pickle sandwiches I've ever tasted.

Mum had a real talent for cooking meals that went a long way and she could do wonders with a pound of mince. Spaghetti Bolognaise, rissoles and meat loaf were some of my favorite mince dishes, and if she had the money this was sometimes served with mashed potatoes, pumpkin, peas and gravy. Our stepfather Bob was an awesome cook, and if his horse racing bets went well he would sometimes treat us to a Sunday roast. These were few and far between, but oh boy, were they good.

When times were tough, before sending us off to school, Mum would heat milk in a saucepan and pour it over white bread sweetened with sugar or jam, and it swelled in our bellies, filling us long enough to get us through until lunch time.

Long before and during our early school years, schools used to provide milk for the students. The milkman would deliver these small glass bottles of milk just before morning recess, and we would all march out like soldiers ready to serve our commanding officer, and God help you if you did anything wrong. If you did, you were immediately sent to the back of the line where there was a good chance that you would miss out.

For flavoured milk we were given straws that had dry powdered flavoring inside of them. Through this you would suck up the white liquid and it miraculously turn into chocolate or strawberry depending on the straw you chose. I'm sure Mum counted on this, along with the sandwich she made for each of us to get us through the day.

She could feed an army on two dollars worth of chips, and a loaf of bread, and even when we had friends over she would include them, even if it meant missing out herself. The chips would come wrapped in newspaper, and she would tear a small piece of paper for each of us and place a few chips on each. Depending on how many kids she had to feed, we would each receive an equal number; usually 6 to 10, and this along with a slice of bread would be our lunch. If we were lucky, we would get cordial to wash it down.

This was a treat usually reserved for weekends, (if Mum had the money), and one day she sent Desley and I to the shop to buy the chips and a loaf of bread. It was fresh out of the bakers oven, and still hot. It smelled so good we started to nibble on it, and by the time we got home we had eaten half the center out of it; I guess we figured she wouldn't notice it as we sat at the table expecting our second helping.

As she put the bread on the cutting board, and began to unwrap it, this revealed the extent of the damage we had done. It was so hollow, she could have slipped her hand in and worn it as a glove, and boy was she pissed. Needless to say, Desley and I were sent to bed on an empty stomach; well maybe not empty, but we went to bed early.

After lunch on the weekends we sometimes found ourselves still hungry, so off we would go to the local parks where dozens of families picnicked, and where we were always guaranteed that some tasty morsel would be left behind. Most of us waited until the picnickers had left before going through the garbage bins, but Gary didn't seem to mind being seen and was usually in the bins before they had a chance to pack up their belongings and leave. He always shared what he found with the rest of us; a half a hamburger, a few chips or whatever. Of course Mum didn't know about this, and I'm sure she would have been mortified had she known.

She was a terrific mother, and one thing we learnt about

Mum was that she never forgot anything, and if you messed up, God help you! She had the patience of a lion waiting in long grass for it's prey to draw near, and rather than chase you around the house, she would bide her time until she thought you had forgotten; and without warning, when you least expected it, she would pounce. This could take up to a week, and by this time, she had lulled you into a false sense of security, and you had forgotten why she was punishing you in the first place.

With every stroke of the cord however, she would remind you why she was teaching you a lesson. One stroke for every word was the norm, and then she would dish out an extra one just for good measure. Her weapons of choice were usually the ironing cord, leather belt or wooden paddle, and for some reason no matter where she was in the house, when she finally caught up with you, one of them was always handy. I'm sure she had several of each strategically placed throughout the house, so she could just grab it.

Gary was like a jackrabbit whenever he got into trouble, and as soon as he knew he was in for it, he would take off as fast as his little legs could carry him. He watched her every move and would dodge her for ages and Mum would be so frustrated with trying to catch him that by the time she did she was at boiling point. In order to get one good swing in and to protect herself from his volley's of kicking, she would restrain him by tying him to the bed; and even though he knew the beating would stop as soon as he cried or apologized, he refused to do either. This upset Mum even more, and the madder she got, and as if she was inflicting corporal punishment on a deserting soldier, the stronger the beating became. Whenever this happened he would withdraw from everything like a hermit and I felt sorry for him.

The thought of having your mouth washed out with soap was enough to make you think twice before uttering obscenities in our house, especially for those who experienced this distasteful form of punishment. Mum would make sure it got into every nook and cranny in your mouth and you would be blowing bubbles for ages after. She would of course apologize as she tucked you into bed and tell you that it was for your own good.

She knew what strings to pull if we were up to no good and to get us to stop fighting, and believe me, we were always getting into trouble when we were growing up. Once when she had been sick and in bed for quite some time, and we had been getting on her nerves, she walked into the kitchen with a sealed envelope in her hand. She placed it on the kitchen cupboard and went back to her room. On the outside of the envelope, she had written the words. "WILL, OPEN ONLY IF I DIE".

Well, it sat there for a few hours before it got the better of Desley and she steamed it open. All she focused on were the words "and to my darling daughter Teresa, I leave my sewing machine". Well, Desley was so pissed because she didn't get it, she stormed out of the house, and as Teresa was the lucky recipient of the sewing machine, she wouldn't talk to her for ages.

Mum had a real talent for decorating and could spot a bargain a mile away. One day she came home with about 50 yards of orange net material and proceeded to make curtains for the entire house. She did a great job, but even to this day, whenever I see the color orange I am reminded of those orange net curtains covering *every single window in the house !*

Although we didn't get much at Christmas, we always had a great time. Mum would decorate the Christmas tree with tinsel and streamers, and if she couldn't get a real tree, she would find a couple of branches and paint them silver. She'd hang the decorations on it that she had collected over the years, and by the time she'd finished with it, you'd swear it came right out of one of those decorating magazines. We made our own Christmas decorations back then and I can remember every year she would save up the foil milk bottle caps and string them along a long piece of twine to hang around the house.

She had a firm hand and a kind heart, and I recall I was forever in her jewelry box, and often admired a large teardrop crystal that hung from a long silver chain. Many times I sat on Mum's bed and emptied her jewelry box out onto the covers to go through her assortment of costume jewelry. I would put all of the pearls together, the diamonds, earrings, bracelets and pendants, and then I would put them all neatly back into their rightful place in her treasure chest.

One year to my amazement I found the crystal and chain I had admired for so long under the Christmas tree as a gift for me. I didn't realize until many years later that it had been a bad year for us, and Mum didn't have enough to buy gifts. Rather than see us go without, she wrapped up some of her own possessions. Of course she borrowed it many times after that, but I didn't mind. Many years after I moved away from home she called me and asked if I still had it. "Of course I did" I told her, and after our conversation, I quickly got it out, dusted it off, and started wearing it again. It now hangs from a special place in our living room where I get to see it every day.

My fondest memory of Mum was of her Christmas plum puddings. They were to die for, and she would get up as early as four o'clock on Christmas day to start her plan of attack. She would mix the ingredients of a recipe ingrained in her memory from years of use, and pour the blend onto pieces of calico. This would be gathered up into a loose ball and tied tightly with string, after which she would lower the pudding into hot water and boil it for several hours, before hanging it out on the clothes-line to cool. To finish the cooking process, just before the Christmas dinner was served she would place the calico wrapped pudding back in the boiling water for another hour, and a small piece would be placed in each bowl, with hot custard poured on the still steaming pudding. It would just melt in your mouth, and it was beautiful. The best part about Christmas was Mum's plum pudding, but we never seemed to get enough.

Mum's Plum Pudding recipe.

4 tablespoons of margarine or butter.
4 tablespoons of sugar.
1 kilo of mixed fruit.
2 cups of self raising flour, or 2 cups of plain flour
and 1 teaspoon of Baking Soda.
2 teaspoons of nutmeg.
2 teaspoons of cinnamon.
¼ to ½ cup of rum.

Mix all ingredients well and pour onto a piece of calico or linen. Gather up and tie into a tight knot, making sure you leave little room for the pudding to swell. Put in a large pot and cover with boiling water. Keep adding boiling water to keep the water level above the pudding, and boil for 4 hours. Hang on line to cool. To reheat, simply drop pudding (still in cloth) into boiling water for approximately one hour, or heat in a microwave. Serve with ice cream or custard. Very Yummy.

Mum was a very conscientious person and regardless of our monetary situation she always tried to have all of us looking clean and tidy. She applied the same rule to herself and often did things at home to save a few pennies. Fifty years ago, home hair colors weren't available in stores like they are today and if you wanted to change the color of your hair you either went to a salon (which of course she couldn't afford), or you made your own concoction. In an effort to change the color of her hair from red to blonde she rubbed a mixture of washing powder and ammonia on her head. She left it on until she thought is was ready, but to her horror, when she tried to wash it out, most of her hair fell out and for the next few weeks she had to wear a scarf to hide her bald patches.

Back in the fifties, we didn't have the luxury of a hot water tap that you could simply turn on to fill the bath, and with so many children to bathe, bath-time was a laborious job for Mum. To heat the water she would light a fire under a 40-gallon boiler, and when it was hot enough, she would cart the water in a bucket, filling the tub twice; once for the girls, and once for the boys. This was an everyday occurrence for her and she always said that this kept her fit enough to keep up with us.

It was always a race to be first in the bath, and with the combination of warm water and weak bladders there was always an uncertainty about the purity of it. As much as Mum tried to make us all go before jumping in, you never knew how many before you had peed in it; I know I did!

Until we were old enough to protest, she would bathe each and every one of us herself. She had a strong hand, and would lather up the face cloth with soap, and scrub us behind the ears so hard, by the time we got out of the bath we looked like we'd just gotten a good whipping. Climbing into the hot soapy bath was like being snug in bed on a cold night, but as the water cooled and the skin on our hands began to wrinkle, the feeling of comfort soon waned, and it was another race to get to one of the few dry towels.

As with baths, our meals were also in two sittings, with the kids eating first, after which the dishes were washed and the table set again for the adults. We advanced to the adult table when an older sibling was leaving home, or on our 12th birthday and for some reason when it was my time to move up, there was a huge fight. I don't know if it was jealousy, or they just didn't want me to leave their ever so dwindling group. I prefer to think it was the latter, but probably not.

We often shared beds in the early days, with at least two of us and sometimes three sleeping head to toe. Of course Mum always put the boys with the boys, and the girls with girls, but it wasn't unusual to have a little sister or brother sneak into bed to snuggle up with you during the night. The departure of an older sibling often meant an improvement in the sleeping arrangements, with the oldest child still remaining at home taking precedence over the younger ones. When we all lived at home, several of us shared bedrooms which often resembled barracks or sleeping quarters at a dormitory, and Mum would hang sheets or blankets between the beds for privacy if both sexes shared the same room.

The first TV in our neighborhood was a real important social event, and all activity in the neighborhood stopped so we could all go down to the local shop after dinner to watch it. Every night at closing time, the shop owner would turn the TV around so those outside under the shop awning could watch it through the large glass pane window. We would all head down early with our folding chairs and blankets to get a prime position, and sit and wait for the main attraction to begin.

Of course it all depended on how Mum's day went, and

if we behaved ourselves she would bathe and feed us early so we could all head down to watch the test patterns. Yes, that's right, test patterns! By the time the shop closed at six and the shop owner turned the TV around for us, that's all we got to see, but oh, was it exciting; or was it the family gatherings that made it so special? The station eventually extended the viewing hours and seeing everything in miniature form in such a small box was a real treat, but I could never figure out how they got everyone through those tiny tubes!

I remember, one Saturday night, sitting with everyone watching a horror movie and afterwards having to walk home in the dark. It was pretty dark by the time the movie had finished and unbeknown to us, one of my older sisters, Dawn, had snuck home, thrown a sheet over her head, and hid behind a bush. As we got nearer to our house she jumped out and scared the living daylights out of us. We all screamed and ran in opposite directions, and Mum was so pissed off with Dawn she chased her halfway up the street, and would have skinned her alive if she had been able to catch her.

The first TV we ever had at home was a coin operated one that gave one hour of viewing for a 2 shilling piece. For sure you would be watching a movie, or Mum would be in the middle of watching the news, and the time would run out. But we had a system in place whenever this happened, and a knife, not just any knife, but the one with a thin curvy blade was used to maneuver the coin back out the bottom of the container. Desley had a real knack for doing this and would be ready to pounce as soon as the time was up.

Once a month, the rental agency would send a guy around to empty the box, and every time he would question the amount of time we watched TV, and the mysterious scratch marks at the bottom of the container. They eventually took the TV back because there was only ever 2 shillings in the container and it wasn't making any money for them.

Back then if you had a TV you were required by law to buy a TV license. This covered the cost of the few channels operating, but to save a few dollars, if she could get away with it, Mum would hide the TV whenever the license inspector came snooping around the house. He usually turned up unannounced, but whenever the neighbors could, they would warn each other as he made his way up the street to collect the licence fee. As soon as Mum was notified of his impending arrival, she developed muscles where I'd never seen them before, and like a woman lifting a car off her dying child, she would pick up the TV, and carry it to the bedroom by herself. More than once she had been caught with an empty table where the TV once stood, so she would fill the void with something else before opening the door.

The inspector was greeted with the usual friendly smile, and she even had the audacity to invite him in, but of course he would decline and go on his way. As soon as the coast was clear however, back came the TV, but of course this time her strength had waned and it took more than one person to carry it out from it's hiding place.

Before colour TV came out, our local electrical shop started selling rolls of coloured film. This was really something to write home about! It was a multi-coloured film that was put on the front of your black and white TV, similar to film you would put on a window, and you had a choice of two varieties. One with a blue top, brown middle and green bottom, and the other with a green top, yellow middle and blue bottom. It was pretty exciting for a while, but the novelty soon wore off having to watch everything with the same color scheme, or a newsreader who looked like he was just about to do a technicolor yawn.

One day a black and white Cocker Spaniel followed us home from the beach, and we convinced Mum that it didn't belong to anyone. We begged her to let us keep it, and called it Cleopatra; that is until we discovered she was a he, and changed his name to Cleo. Cleo was a very energetic Spaniel that peed on anything and everything in sight. Whenever he lost sight of us, he'd start sniffing and peeing, until he finally found us; at which stage he would pee again just from the sheer joy of finding us.

On one particular day, we had been down at the beach for quite some time when Cleo wandered off, and the next thing we hear this guy yelling and swearing at the top of his lungs. Apparently, Cleo wasn't being too fussy about where he was peeing, and had cocked his leg on a baby in a bouncer-net, peed in it's mouth, and caused the child to get quite a mouthful. Needless to say, when the guy started yelling out for the owner of the dog to make themselves known, we didn't know who they were either, the bastards !

Because of Cleo's tendency to relieve himself where he saw fit and embarrassing us in the process, I recall many times taking him down to the beach and planning our escape when we thought he wasn't looking. But no matter how many times we tried he would sense our departure, and if there was no chance of him catching up to us, he would simply sit down and cry so loud that he would attract everyone's attention and we had no choice but to wait for him.

Trips to the beach were often hazardous undertakings, especially when we had Cleo with us. He would "dig to China" trying to find crabs, and the beach looked like a battle zone by the time we left. Before leaving to go home we would have to fill in all the holes for fear of someone breaking a leg, or losing their kid.

Although we had Cleo for nearly three years, Mum was always threatening to get rid of him. He had those big hound dog eyes, and between them and us begging, we always saved him for another day. That is, until the day he ate her much beloved blue budgie Sam. Mum loved that bird, and would take him out of his cage every day so he could sit on her shoulder and nibble on her ear. She taught him to sing and kiss, and whenever we got visitors she would proudly show him off to everyone.

One day she went out, and although we knew Cleo wasn't allowed in the house, somehow he got in, and as it was rain-ing we let him stay inside to keep dry. Forgetting Cleo was in the house, one of the kids let Mum's budgie out of the cage, and the next thing Cleo had it between his teeth with six of us trying to pry his mouth open before he swallowed it. Cleo ran out of the house with us in tow, but he had done the damage before we could pry Sam from his jaws. We buried what was left of Sam in a shoe box, along with a pair of rosary beads, but we knew there would be hell to pay when Mum got home.

Gary got the bright idea of replacing Sam with another budgie that looked just like him, so we all pooled the few pennies we had and Gary, Desley and I headed down to the pet shop. We found another blue budgie and took it home so Mum would be none the wiser, and everything seemed ok, until she got him out of his cage, and he bit her on the lip when she tried to kiss him. She also noticed the congealed blood from where we had clipped it's wings too short, but the dead giveaway was the blue feathers that were still stuck to Cleo's coat and on the living room carpet. She was very upset, to the point of being scary.

The next morning Mum was hanging out the washing in the back yard, and found the rosary beads that had been dug up by Cleo. It was bad enough that he had murdered her precious Sam, but to dig up the body and finish it off, well that was the last straw. He knew he was in deep shit, and stayed clear of her for ages.

He followed us everywhere and I'm sure Mum prayed each time we left the house that we would return without him. One day, not long after he had finished Sam off, she asked Dawn and her fiance Laurie, to take Cleo for a walk and get rid of him. They decided to throw him off the deep end of the Scarborough Pier, and as Cleo wasn't a strong swimmer, they were pretty certain that he wouldn't make it. They headed down to the pier long before we got out of bed, and after making sure no one was looking, Laurie quickly tossed Cleo into the water, and he promptly started heading back home with Dawn. As they were nearing the other end of the pier however, an old lady started yelling out about a drowning dog.

Dawn and Laurie were the only other people around, so it was a little difficult for them to ignore her and before he knew it, Laurie was jumping in to rescue Cleo from his watery grave. When they got back to shore, Cleo was so excited about Laurie coming to his rescue, he almost licked him to death and Mum thought she was seeing things, as all three of them walked in the yard with Laurie and Cleo still dripping wet from their adventure.

No matter who was up first in the house, Cleo was there to greet them at the door. Even if it meant a kick in the gut, his tail was constantly wagging and he always had a smile on his face. Yet, it seems that Mum wasn't the only one trying to get rid of him. One morning we awoke with Cleo nowhere in sight, and we soon found him lying at the bottom of the steps, as sick as a dog. He was always digging holes in the neighbours gardens and pissing them off, and Mum figured that someone had thrown poison bait over the fence and Cleo had swallowed it. Even though he had rejected some of the poison during the night, he was still suffering.

When we found him, he had ant's crawling all over him and we had to clear them from his eyes and mouth to make him more comfortable. We carried him to the laundry and laid him on a blanket and waited, but by the end of the day it was obvious he wasn't going to make it. Mum decided to put him out of his misery and proceeded to pour a whole bottle of sleeping tablets down his throat. We all said our good-byes, and as sad as it was, we could see this was the best thing to do.

The next morning there was a commotion at the back door and we found Cleo healthier than ever, jumping up on everyone and crying so loudly I thought Mum was going to kick him back down the steps. That morning he was allowed in the house, and although she tried not to show her emotions, even

Mum was pleased he was back.

He was a very friendly dog, and as he did with us three years earlier he went home with another family from the beach. I have a feeling that he was a type of nomad and when he got sick of living in the one place, he just packed up his bags and moved on. Mind you, knowing that any day could likely be your last was probably enough of an incentive to make anyone want to move on to greener pastures.

Mum was a strong believer in old remedies, and firmly believed that a good shit to clean your bowels out would fix just about anything. Every Sunday afternoon, we would all stand in line to take our teaspoon of castor oil, which was, and probably still is the foulest tasting stuff I've ever tasted, but a sure fire way of giving you the runs. Sometimes, if she had the money, she would sweeten the castor oil with a little jam or sugar, but no matter how she disguised it, it tasted disgusting. Sunday afternoon was like standing in a dunny lineup at a Rugby League grand final, and pity help the poor bastard last in line. If you haven't tried it, give it a go, but just make sure you don't make any plans for a few hours.

Once when she wasn't feeling well she started to get sores on her body, and a huge carbuncle formed under her arm. She became quite sick with it, and went to the doctor who promptly told her that she was getting these sores because she was malnourished from not eating properly. A good old remedy for boils and carbuncles was a soap and sugar poultice, so Mum mixed a little soap and sugar into a paste, wacked it on the boil, and covered it for a few days. This had a miraculous way of drawing out all the pus and bad germs, and it soon healed better than any doctor's antibacterial remedy.

> *Soap and Sugar poultice.*
> *In a small bowl, mix a tablespoon of pure Sunlight soap (must be pure soap) and a sprinkle of sugar. Add a little water (½ teaspoon) and mix to a thick paste. Apply to a bandage and cover the wound but make sure you change the bandage daily. Good for boils, carbuncles or any other infection. Do not put near eyes.*

Whenever we got a cut or injury of some kind, out would come Mum's medicine box which she stored under her bed. In it she stockpiled a number of items including bandages of varying widths and lengths. It was too expensive for her to buy manufactured bandages, especially with such a large family, so she would make her own by ripping up an old sheet. She would sterilize the strips in boiling water before hanging them out to dry and then roll them up and include them with the other first aid provisions. On many occasions we used strips of sheeting to curl our hair, and as funny as we looked when doing this, the end result was quite satisfying.

Another necessary item in Mum's first aid supply box was the ever dreaded iodine bottle. This ocher coloured mixture went on just about anything, and as much as she tried to convince us that it was for our own good, we could never understand how something so good, could be so painful. Her favorite cure for cold sores was perfume, and like iodine the pain it caused was enough for you to not want to complain about your ailments in the first place. There was no getting away from it though, because as soon as the sore became apparent on your lip, out would come the perfume bottle and cotton wool. The boys had it worse than the girls however, as they not only had to endure the pain as we did, but for the rest of the day they went about their day smelling like Tabu.

Mother's Day was near, but we didn't have anything for her, or any money to buy her a present. Mum loved gardening and Gary got the idea of a bench for her to sit on in the backyard, so he snuck out after dark with Bart and Teresa to see what they could find. The nearest bus stop was a fair distance from the house, but regardless, they were determined to bring her back a bench for her garden. They found a bench they liked and proceeded to carry it back home, and every time a car came by they would sit down and pretend they were waiting for a bus. At one point a bus even stopped to pick them up, but they said they were just resting and the driver closed the door and took off. At least they weren't lying. When they finally got it home they wacked a coat of paint on it, and put it in the middle of the garden in the back yard. It was a joy to behold, and even though the paint hadn't dried, Mum was overjoyed when she woke the next morning to see her new garden bench.

Because real estate agents were reluctant to lease to such a large family, whenever we had to move it was always a challenge for Mum to find a house for us. To eliminate this problem she would only take a few of us to the agency with her, or she would tell them that she only had six kids. Whenever they came to collect the rent, they would often be left scratching their head, because of the different faces, but Mum would simply laugh it off, and tell them that the cousins were visiting.

Back then, the real estate agencies sent a rent collector around every two weeks to collect what was owed, and many times when she didn't have the money, she would tell all of us to be quiet until he left. On one of these occasions when she again didn't have the rent money for him, she sent Dawn (who was around 12 at the time) to answer the door and tell him she wasn't home. Mum stood behind the door coaxing Dawn as she opened it and when asked by the collector "is your mother home?", Dawn said "no". This would normally send him on his way, however, when he asked "what time would she be back", on hearing this Dawn looked behind the door and said to Mum "He said, what time will you be back?". She was so embarrassed and came out from behind the door with a tale of them playing hide and seek. I'm sure he didn't believe her, but gave her extra time to pay the rent anyway.

The Brisbane Exhibition is a large annual family event that exhibits livestock and horticulture in one big festival; with rides and junk food being the main attraction for the younger generation. One year, we were fortunate enough to go and sat with the rest of the crowd watching the police precision drivers show their expertise in this rather sensational event. When it was finished, the announcer asked the crowd to be patient and remain seated as they had something special coming up. As we sat patiently, they drove a big black car into the center of the arena, and the announcer called for the largest family to make themselves known. Mum and our Dad, did a quick head count to make sure we were all there and yelled out as loud as they could "Fourteen".

As much as I wanted to hide under the seat, the thought of a new car was too exciting, and we all went down to the center with Mum and Dad smiling from ear to ear. They thought for sure they had won, until a family of fifteen stood up to claim the prize. As we were the second largest family, we received a crate (twenty four bottles) of Coca Cola, which I'm sure was an afterthought for the judges as they hadn't expected two such large families. As we sat in the middle of the arena waiting for the formalities to end, Dad opened the bottles and we downed them as if it was the last supper. Desley and I soon got the willies and had to squat on the grass to pee in the middle of the arena, all the time praying that none of our schoolmates were in the crowd watching.

Mum and Dad had great parties, which were often unplanned when friends would inevitably stay longer after dropping by for a short visit. Their visits turned into larger gatherings, with lots of singing around the old piano, but as soon as eight o'clock came, the kids were sent to bed, and the adults continued partying until the wee hours of the morning. When we thought it was safe, we would sneak out of our beds, lie in the darkened hallway, and listen to stories that we had heard time and time again. But no matter how many times we had heard them, they always seemed so real, and we couldn't wait until we were old enough to take part in this special gathering.

As certain as we were that the sun would rise, someone would suggest a seance, and with this we would all scurry back to our beds. Not because we were frightened, but we knew that Mum would be checking the hallway before the seance started, to make sure none of us were up. As soon as the all clear was given however, we would be back in the hallway with our ears pressed against the wall waiting with bated breath for it to start.

Each person would sit around the big oval table, and so the supernatural being had a way of passing through each of them, they would place their hands palms down with their fingers touching each other. To make the atmosphere even more scarier the lights were turned out, and a candle lit, and as the night progressed and many hours of drinking the bottled variety, the other kind of spirits took over, and the stories became more and more about the power of the mind than fact.

The very table the seance was being conducted at, had a mysteriously strange and frightening way about it and no matter how quiet we were, it could tell when we were in the hallway. It could hear the slightest sound, and I recall many times during my childhood, being chased to bed by the spirits that overtook the minds of those sitting at this table. I don't know why everyone thought it was so funny, but we would all run off to bed screaming and pull the blankets over our heads for fear of being grabbed. Of course, I now know better, but as a 6 year old being chased to bed during a seance was a frightening experience, but oh, what an experience.

I remember when we were young, Mum once had a Pianola that you operated by pumping the pedals with your feet to activate the keys. The operator would play without touching the keys with their hands and the rolls of perforated paper would go from one spool to another. The younger kids thought this was an amazing trick. Each of us took turns playing the Pianola with the older kids sitting on the floor pumping the foot lever for the younger ones whose feet couldn't reach the pedals.

Back in the forties and fifties dance halls were prevalent and a popular stomping ground for the livelier set. The Jitter Bug, Waltz, Two Step and Jive were some of Mum's favorite dance steps, and the Saturday night dance sessions were the perfect place to not only meet people, but also show the flair she had developed during her many years of dancing on stage when she was young.

This was a time when fashion accessories included the six inch spiked heels, and women were required by law to wear girdles and petticoats. They were hot and uncomfortable and starched with a mixture of sugar and water. Even when I was a child I remember Mum starching our Sunday best using this method.

She was a great dancer and it was at one of these dances

during the forties that she met two gentlemen by the names of Bill and Clem. They were great guys who lived together, but because of their special relationship, which was frowned on by the public back then, they kept their personal life a secret.

Clem, who many times was Mum's dance partner, was often thought to be her lover, but this couldn't have been further from the truth. A friendship developed that has lasted to this day. Bill and Clem became our unofficial uncles, and for as long as I can remember, took part in many of our family gatherings.

In 1969 while in her late forties, Mum met and married a man almost 30 years younger. He was a Canadian guy traveling around Australia, and as soon as they saw each other, it was love at first sight, and although there was a big difference in their ages, it didn't deter a relationship from developing. Not long after they were married Barry adopted the three youngest boys still living at home, and early in their relationship, they traveled around Australia with them. This was an exciting time for everyone, and although it was a great adventure, the boys missed out on things such as close friendships that develop from being in one place.

After traveling from one town to another, Mum had enough of the nomadic life, however Barry wanted to continue traveling, and although their feelings for each other never waned, the difference in their ages soon became apparent. They soon settled down to the humdrum of normal married life on the Gold Coast, which was a far cry from the adventurous life they had lived the first few years of their relationship, and while Mum was content with the familiarities of this, Barry started to get itchy feet.

Every Friday afternoon, Mum's routine included the weekly grocery shopping, after which Barry would drive by on his way home from work to pick her up. One day however, she waited for what seemed like hours, and was surprised to see Gary driving the three boys to collect her instead of Barry. Unbeknown to Mum, when the boys got home from school Victor had found a note addressed to her from Barry on the kitchen table, and as Gary lived nearby they told him about it. After reading the note, he realized it was a Dear Jane letter in which Barry expressed his undying love for her, but the desperate need to experience more of life than he could in one place.

Mum was devastated and the whole family gathered around to support and console her, and while she understood his desire for adventure, she couldn't understand that it was stronger than his desire to be with her. She dwelled on his disappearance for quite some time, and eventually moved on with her life, but she never got over him completely. She dated other men from time to time but she never allowed herself to get too serious about them. Certainly not enough to share a life together.

In 1995, 20 years after they parted, Barry who now lives in Canada started writing to Mum. His letters would always travel via my older sister Coral, and she would in turn pass them on to Mum, however it's only recently that they have started communicating with each other directly. Again and again, Barry has expressed his desire to see her, but she has begged him not to visit. I have a feeling it's not that she doesn't want to see him, but rather because the differences in their ages would be more apparent now than before. At 84, she is now in a wheelchair and going through the usual symptoms familiar with growing old, while he at my age of 54 is still in the prime of his life. But given the history, I wonder if they did get together again, if he would find her just as beautiful as he once did?

CHAPTER THREE

Mum's own memories of our childhood.

YOUR DAD AND I WERE married on June 4th 1939, when I was eighteen, and he was nineteen, and we had some funny times. One day when Coral, Dawn, Billy, and Teresa were little, and Barton was a baby, Coral showed me how to harness up the horse and sulky which I had never done before, so we could surprise Dad and be waiting for him at the abattoir when he finished work. Well, you should have seen the look on his face when he came out and saw us waiting at the gate. "Don't you ever do this to me again you silly bitch" he said on sight. "We were lucky we survived the ride," he said, "as the harness was put on wrongly."

On another day, we were on our way to his work and

was going over the Tingalpha Creek Bridge, (I was pregnant with you Wendy, so you were there in a way). Anyway, some electricity workers were putting up new lines and one of them farted and the horse took fright and bolted. Well there I was, standing up trying to stop the horse and looking more like a Roman in a chariot with my big dress blowing than a pregnant woman. We went for miles before I managed to stop it and I have to tell you I never tried that again, it scared the living daylights out of me.

We went everywhere in a horse and sulky back then and once when we were going on a picnic we got into a real mess. We always had our gate closed so the animals couldn't get out and Coral went on to open it and we were to pick her up when she closed the gate once the horse and sulky got through. Outside of our little farmlet, there was no guttering and the ground was rough and worn away from where the water came rushing down the hill whenever it rained and crumbled away the sides. Our horse made for the gate at a fast pace and went straight over the washed out gutter, and the pies I had made for the picnic, plus the cold meat and tomato sandwiches, flew all over the kids, and with a bump I ended up on the back of the horses neck, holding on for dear life. Needless to say there was no picnic that day.

One day, we decided to go to Wellington Point which was a popular swimming area about fifteen miles from home. Dad had no coat on, and the kids were in their togs and shorts, and after eating lunch the sky started to darken over. We were in for a big storm, and all we had to protect ourselves was an old army blanket in the back of the sulky, so Dad told me to put it over us while he sat driving. We went for what seemed like miles then pulled up all of a sudden, and as I stuck my head out from under the blanket to ask what all the noise was about, I noticed we were under a shop awning. It's funny now when I think of it, but at the time it was quite scary and very embarrassing. The horse was trying to protect itself from the rain and he had his head over the counter looking right into the shop, and the customers were running out into the rain with fright.

Once when we were pretty desperate and short of food in the house, Dad took a friend of his to raid a chook farm. They took off about 9pm, but they were home empty handed within the hour. You see, his friend was a real dill and when your Dad was showing him how to grab the chooks, the farmer came out with a gun and Dad and the friend took off. They ran and kept going until the friend fell down a well, bloody idiot! They kept quiet until the farmer stopped chasing, then Dad helped him out of the well and they came home empty handed.

I've never got over your sister Jacqueline Dianne's death. Healthy one minute, hospital and death the next. Nana had given her her first ice cream, and later that day she went into convulsions, one after the other. We took her to Moorooka Ambulance Station and they rushed her to the Mater Children's Hospital, however back in them days we couldn't stay with her.

Now days if something happens to a baby one of the parents can stay with them, but back then it was against hospital rules. We went home and returned again at 7am the next morning, but they wouldn't tell us anything and they wouldn't let us see her. They sent us home again, but I maintain to this day she was already dead and they just didn't want to tell us to our face. There was a message waiting for us when we got home saying she had died. I was seven months pregnant with Billy at the time, and it was so tragic as she was a beautiful baby. Fourteen months old and so much like her sister Coral. I will never forget going to the crematorium in the horse and buggy with her little white coffin on the back seat between your Dad and me.

When your father and I split up he took Billy, Barton, and Gary for a "holiday" to Nana Clarke's place in Brisbane. At the time we were living at Ballina and your father was living with his new lady Phyllis, who is now his widow. Anyway, Bart and Gary wouldn't call Phyllis "Mum", so they were promptly returned while Billy was bribed with a watch to stay with them. Because they traveled around so much and we couldn't trace him, we didn't see Billy again for about 10 years, but he found us when he was grown up and we were living on Bribie Island.

We were a happy and close family and we're all still very close today, but we lost Billy in a house fire a few years ago and I was devastated when I found out. My third son Gary, was killed in a car accident when he was 34 and when I found out I was sitting on the couch in my lounge room when my daughter Teresa came to the door. As soon as I saw her I knew something was wrong but I could never have guessed it was this bad. December 2001, and I just had the best Christmas ever. I went to Carol's as you know, and many of our family were there. We had a wonderful time; champagne and oysters for breakfast and a seafood dinner. A great many of Carol's relatives on Steve's side of the family were there also and there were kids galore. The pool was popular and it was great to see everyone happy and having so much fun.

I have outlived three of my children, and I'm praying I go before Carol. I have a feeling she will outlive me, as she has so much determination; I pray she will anyway, because the thought of losing another child is too much to bear.

Note: Carol passed away five months after Mum wrote this.

CHAPTER FOUR

My Memories of my Father,
William Henry Clarke
(Born February 13,1920)

I REMEMBER LITTLE OF MY REAL FATHER, except that he was always trying to make ends meet. He worked a variety of jobs, and when we spent some time on a dairy farm, he used to milk all of the cows by hand. He was used to hard yakka, and he was a butcher by trade, but I only know this because it's written on my birth certificate.

Dad drove taxies for a while but lost his right arm one day while he was out on a job. I was told a semi-trailer carrying a huge grader overtook the double line, and the blade of the grader which was hanging over the side of the trailer caught Dad's arm; he had it resting on the rolled down window, and it was sliced clean off. He was often out of work or on strike, and he and Mum would have to make do with what they could. On many of these occasions, Dad's father, Granddad Clarke would ride his bike around to the house with a bag full of food to help us out. Good old Granddad.

My parents split up when I was around 5 and at the time we lived in a huge army surplus tent that had rooms divided by hanging blankets. The girls slept in one section, the boys in the other, and Mum and Dad had another section blanketed off. One night we could hear giggling outside the tent, and were shocked to discover that several boys had fought for prime viewing positions to watch the older girls silhouettes while they undressed by the light of the lanterns. There was hell to pay, and Dad tanned their hides, and threatened to lynch them if they ever came around again. You could get away with tanning hides fifty years ago, without the fear of being sued.

I remember, we used to go on lots of picnics when we lived with Dad, but that changed when our stepfather came on the scene. It wasn't long after we moved into this tent that Mum and Dad separated, and we didn't see Dad for a long time after that. He came back into my life many years later when I was married and had my first son Jason. Dad was living not far from us on a farm with his wife Phyllis, and my husband thought it would be a great idea if he took me to visit him. We played house and were respectful of each other, but because my father hadn't been a part of my life for such a long time I could never foster the closeness that develops with years of growing up together. I recall only seeing him a couple of times after that, however my oldest sister Coral never stopped corresponding with Dad or visiting him, and did so until he passed away in 1997.

CHAPTER FIVE

My memories of our step-father, Bob
(Born in 1924)

T MAY SEEM CONFUSING, but we called our real father Dad, as well as our stepfather. Our stepfather was with us for almost fourteen years from when I was around five, and at his insistence we started calling him Dad shortly after he came on the scene. Most of my memories of a father figure are of him when I called him Dad, however throughout the book he is also called Bob.

I realize I have three adult males in my memories; our real father Dad, our stepfather whom we also called Dad, and Bob. Throughout this journal, whenever the immoral side of our stepfather came out, I called him Bob (not his real name) and he was the one I didn't want to recognize as a father figure.

When he became Bob, I thought of him as an intruder in the family, and the nasty side of our stepfather didn't deserve recognition, but the gentle side of him, the one that I recognized as Dad, did.

He was quite good looking and resembled the 1950's actor Victor Mature, and he was a real ladies man, and a bit of a casanova. He was also a thief, and I remember one day when he came home with a large quantity of truck tyres that he had stolen. He was selling them cheap to some of the locals, and it didn't take long before word got out about the tyres that were going for a song.

We lived out of town on a farm at the time, and when he heard that the police were looking for him, he hid up in the attic. He did this for several weeks and Mum would pass food up to him during the day and sometimes he would come down through the trapdoor that led to the attic, and join us for dinner; or what there was of it. He managed to elude the police for a few weeks before being captured, but I remember Mum once saying that she wished he'd get caught as we were better off without him; at least we had more food between us.

She didn't like the fact that she was putting us in danger by harboring a criminal, but she was torn between her loyalty to him, and protecting us from a situation she couldn't get out of.

Our oldest sister Coral, who was 16 at this time had just started dating a young policeman, and every day he would pick her up from her job at the pub and drive her home. For fear of being caught, Mum and Bob forbade her from bringing him in the yard, let alone up to the front door; so she would get him to drop her off at the gate or down the road. On one of Bob's excursions from the attic we were all seated around the kitchen table waiting for Mum to serve breakfast when there was a rather loud knock at the door, and without warning Bob jumped under the table.

No matter how hard-up we were, Mum always insisted on the linen tablecloth on the table and the table properly set for meals, and with the length of the tablecloth, and all of those legs, I'm sure he thought this would be the perfect hiding place. Mum answered the door and in walked four burly police officers, including the one who had been dating Coral. I could see the embarrassment in Coral's eyes, but at the time she didn't realize that she had been set up, and he was just dating her to get into the house.

After searching the house, including the attic, they were convinced that Bob was nowhere to be seen, and if it wasn't for the smaller kids peeking under the table as the police officers made their way through the kitchen, he would have gotten away with it. He was arrested and jailed for two years for theft and selling stolen goods.

When he went to jail, Mum would make weekly trips to the Wacol Prison to take Bob his weekly package of tobacco, soap and anything special she made for him. (No, there were no cakes with saws in them), but on days that Mum didn't feel like going, she would send Teresa instead. Teresa would sometimes take me, but I didn't like going, so Desley and I would take turns. None of us really liked going so the visits were always short. To make best of it, Teresa sometimes took a few cents out of Mum's purse to buy lollies.

I remember another time, when we were still living on the farm when I was around 7 or 8, and he came in the house with a heap of stuff. There was a lot of lingerie and other woman's things and he asked us to pick something, but we didn't realize at the time that they had been stolen, and I picked a pink satin petticoat. Not long after that the police came again and went into our attic. They brought down more stuff including necklaces and earrings.

Bob went back to jail and although it was hard without the breadwinner, life went on at the farm. It was really difficult for Mum and at times we lived on nothing but potatoes, bread and milk, or bread cooked in dripping for dinner with a cup of tea. Going to bed on an empty stomach was common, but Mum always made sure she saw to us before looking after herself. It was around this time, that I woke one evening to the sound of strangers talking in the kitchen. As we often had people dropping in I didn't think too much about it, but on this particular night I could hear a nervous tone in Mum's voice and I decided to sneak up the hallway to see who it was.

As I peeked between the crack in the kitchen door, I noticed two strangers and to my horror, a gun on the kitchen table. I inadvertently made a noise and Coral looked up, grabbed me by the arm, and took me back to my bed, and although I was so scared I stayed awake all night. I don't know what happened but they were gone the next morning when I got up to go to school. Apparently, Bob had told his jail-bird friends that Mum would look after them and give them a safe hiding place if they ever needed one.

Mum always said that a change was as good as a holiday so she was forever moving the furniture around in the house, and I recall many times Bob coming home late after a night of boozing at the pub, and ricocheting off the walls and pieces of furniture as he made his way through the house. Getting from the front door to the bedroom was bad enough when you're drunk, without someone placing obstacles in your way! It was a real struggle for him and I could hear each and every step and injury along the way.

When we moved to Bribie Island, the house we moved into was missing the front verandah, and the two french doors opened to nowhere. When he had too much to drink, Bob would often open these to use as a watering hole, and more than once he stepped out to relieve himself, and landed on the grass 9 feet below. I can see him now, propping himself up against the side of the door with one arm, as he tried to guide his only free hand down his trouser pants.

It wasn't unusual to see Mum with a black eye or bruises on her face or arm from where he had grabbed her too tightly. During these times she wore her makeup heavy and the house was so quiet you could hear a pin drop. The silence was deafening, and we would all tip-toe around the house and did whatever Mum wanted just to make her happy.

I recall one night when they had a big fight and when she woke the next morning, she had a black eye and wasn't feeling well. Their fights were usually about money and he was always trying to convince her that he could double or triple what little they had on the Saturday horse races. Mum hated the horses and preferred the money they had in their hand, to the sure thing he had been told about by one of his gambling buddies.

Regardless, he usually got his way and every Saturday morning he would take a walk down to the TAB to place his bets. The radio would be turned up as loud as it could go, and he would listen to each of his horses come in. Depending on how they did, his mood would change like a chameleon throughout the day, and Mum would adjust hers to suite. One minute he was up and the next he was down, and if he lost he would take it out on her every time.

One day his horses were losing and he tried to convince Mum to give him her last $20 but she wouldn't, and even though this was all she had to get us through the following week, he didn't care and he tried every maneuver to get it from her. The gently persuasive approach was used first, but when that failed he used the strong-arm approach. She finally caved in, but he got so pissed off with her he threw it back in her face and stormed out the house. She hung on to the $20 as if her life depended on it. She proceeded to prepare dinner on the wooden stove, but her mind was obviously somewhere else and when she opened the door of the stove to stoke the fire, without thinking she tossed the $20 into the flames.

It was only a split second before she realized what she had done and her hand went in to retrieve what was left of it, but it was too late. She received bad burns to her hand and no sympathy from Bob when he came home later that night drunk. "The bastard" she said, "he always seemed to find enough for his gambling and drinking"

I shared a small bedroom with my two sisters, Teresa and Desley. It had two windows, one of which looked into the neighbors yard and the other onto the enclosed porch that Mum had fashioned into a couple of bedrooms for the boys. One Saturday, while Teresa was at work, I had been trying on some of her clothes and make up for quite some time and I danced in front of the mirror rather pleased with the outcome. As I spun around listening to my favorite Beatle song, I noticed someone looking at me through the curtain. I don't know how long Bob had been there but he got a shock when he realized I had seen him and he quickly disappeared. As I had gone through several changes of clothing I knew he had seen everything and I felt so embarrassed. He managed to hide this darker side of himself so well that we often forgot about it, until an opportunity loomed and kindled another chance for him.

Although I had lots of boyfriends, they always had me home on time after a date and very rarely did they try anything with me. I have a feeling though that it was those deep

meaningful words of wisdom that Dad passed on to my suit-
ors as they walked me out to their car, that had something to
do with it. I never knew if he was going to deliver the long or
the short version of the possible repercussions of going below
my waist line, but it usually depended on whether or not he
had been drinking.

If he was sober, he tended to use the longer version which
consisted of inviting them in to meet the rest of the family. He
put them through a rather lengthy interrogation process that
any countryman would be proud of, and would have made the
strongest give way under mental and emotional pressure.

On the other hand, if he'd been drinking, he treated them
more like his drinking buddies and as they walked me to their
car, he would deliver the short version of his illuminating
speech. My dates were never very long, but I have a feeling
Dad's message, "Keep your legs together" is still ringing in
their ears. This by the way wasn't delivered in a soft spoken
tone, but rather that of someone making a proclamation with a
megaphone as we made our way to the car.

Mum and Bob separated a year after we moved to the Gold
Coast, and when he moved out he took Carol, Shane and Victor with him. They moved not far from Mum, so the kids could
still visit, but as I was now married I didn't see him much after
that.

CHAPTER SIX

My memories of my oldest sister Coral
(Born in 1939)

I GREATLY ADMIRE MY OLDEST SISTER CORAL, who to me always
seemed so wise. She's one of those people who can do anything with their hands, and although she left school at the
age of 12, and had no formal training, she had a great eye for
detail when it came to fashion and design.

Coral was a great seamstress, and was instrumental in
not only altering all our clothes as they were handed down
from one sibling to the other, but she also made many of our
costumes for plays during our early school years. She was always there for the many different milestones in our lives from
our debutante, to our wedding and bridesmaids dresses, she

gussied us up. She seemed to know everything about anything and to this day she is still a great source of information.

Because Coral was the eldest in the family, she was often responsible for looking after us and making sure we kept out of trouble; God help us if we didn't. She was also responsible for doing all of the dishes until we were old enough to help out, and because Mum insisted on complete table settings for everyone, there was always plenty to do. Our parents were very strict when it came to dating boys, and Coral was forever under a watchful eye and a tight curfew. Any time she went out, she had a chaperone and if she was one minute past the deadline, God help her and the poor bastard who brought her home late.When she was old enough, Coral started going out with Mum and they were often mistaken for sisters. They were both very attractive, and this at times caused jealousy and competitiveness between them, but I felt sorry for Coral because I'm sure she only ever wanted to be treated like a daughter. She and Mum always looked so beautiful whenever they got dressed up, and I can still smell the perfume they drenched their bodies in before leaving the house.

Coral had a fabulous figure and she was very striking and reminded me of one of those movie stars from the fifties or sixties waiting for the man of her dreams to sweep her off her feet. I wonder where she would be now if such a thing had happened. Well, I guess it did because she's still happily married to the same man she married over 41 years ago when she was 21.

Because of the 11 years difference in our age, my memories of Coral are few and far between, but what little I do remember has effected my life in a positive manner, and I will be forever grateful for this.

CHAPTER SEVEN

Coral's own memories of her childhood

MY MEMORIES AS FAR BACK AS I can remember started when I was around 3½, when I remember being at the South Brisbane Railway Station with Mum waiting for Dad to come home on leave from "World War Two". He was in his sailors uniform, and Mum said every sailor I saw after that I called daddy, which I'm sure was very embarrassing for her at the time.

After the war ended in 1945, Jacquelyn was born but died only 14 months later. When I was 6, we lived in a tent as many of the returned servicemen did because they had no jobs. Billy was the apple of Dad and Mum's eye, and poor Dawn was always sick and very tiny for her age. We discovered she had some lung disease and also had to have one of her kidneys removed, but then she grew and put on weight and her health improved.

Teresa was born when I was 8 when we lived at Seven Hills and it was at that time that Mum and Dad bought 6 acres of land at Gumdale. We only lived there for a short time, but I do remember some funny times when Mum was pregnant with Bart and back in those days we went everywhere in a horse and sulky.

One day, we were on our way to Wellington Point and the harness broke, so Dad fixed it up with a bit of string and wire. Mum had all the food in a box on the floor and two custard tarts on the little seat between her and Dad. Dawn, Billy, Teresa and I sat on the floor of the sulky and as Dad drove out of the gate and over the gutter, the harness broke again and Mum ended up on the horses back. Thank God she was a quiet one, the horse that is! We all ended up with our lunch and custard tarts all over us.

Another time, Mum wanted to surprise Dad and asked me to help her harness the horse and sulky, and off we went to Cannon Hill where he worked. On the way, along the main road one of the linesmen working on the electricity wires, "let one drop," and the horse bolted with us kids all screaming and Mum standing up trying to pull up the horse. She finally got it to stop and when we made it to Dad's work, boy was he surprised, and really, really mad."You silly bitch" he said, "you could have killed everyone. You've got the harness on back to front". Needless to say, I got a wack across the head as I had showed Mum how to put it on.

When I was around 11, we moved to Camp Muckley at Archiefield. It was an old U.S. Army Camp and you (Wendy), were a baby at the time. I remember one Mother's Day, when we had no money and Mum had bought a sand ring cake, (sponge with a hole in the middle). Dawn and I decided to sneak over to the Abo's place and pinch some flowers from their garden for Mum. It was pretty late and it was about 200 yards to the community baths and toilets, so Dawn and I were on our bellies, crawling back through the long grass with the flowers. The next thing, out comes old fat Nana from next door, and she decides to squat in the grass for a pee right next to me. Even though she never saw us, she was so close I got peed on, and even some of the flowers copped it. When we got back, we divided the flowers up and used some of them on the cake for Mother's Day, YUK. Oh well, what you don't know won't hurt ya!

Desley was born whilst we were at Camp Muckley and I remember we were always broke and Mum and Dad were always stealing food for us. Dad and a friend, were getting chooks one night and Dad told his friend to, "grab them by the throat and run". There they were, running like hell with chooks in each hand, when all of a sudden Dad's friend disappears down a well still holding on to the chooks. The farm owner heard the ruckus and came out firing but didn't catch them. After a while all Dad could hear was "HELP"!! coming from the dry well. There was his friend down the well, still clutching the chooks. He got him out but ended up coming home empty handed.

Another time, Dad was getting us some watermelons for Christmas and while someone pinched the melons, he thought he'd distract the property owners by knocking on the door to ask where Bill Clarke lived. It turned out to be an old mate he used to go drinking with (when he had a quid) and Dad pretended he was just playing a joke and that he was just calling in to say hi. His mate told Dad about the bastards who had been pinching his melons and that he had set a trap for them. Needless to say, we didn't get any melons that year, at least not from that farm.

I left school when I was twelve and started work in a cake shop when I was thirteen, then a dress shop when I was fourteen. I never had pocket money, but Mum always made sure we were dressed clean and tidy and had neat hair and clean shoes (with cardboard innersoles). I thought we were pretty well off really for a big family.

I was about 13 when Gary was born and the 11 of us moved into a house at Carina. A real house, not a hut or tent, but a real house with walls and four bedrooms. This was the first time I guess that I noticed that Mum and Dad were having marital problems. Even though they always fought, I never thought there was anything wrong with it and I just thought all parents carried on like that. Even when I was small, I don't ever remember them not arguing, so to me it was normal. We used to hide whenever Mum and Dad had a fight as they got quite physical.

Carol was born at Carina and she was a little sweetie, but I never seemed to have enough time for her. We all had our share of jobs to do around the house and because I was the oldest, I was often responsible for the table and doing the dishes, because the other kids were small. I remember one time Mum had told me to get started on cleaning up the dishes, and I had to go to the outhouse (toilet). I was there for about ½ an hour and when I got back it was all done. I thought this was great and I could pull that one off again, so about a week later I got a lamp and some comics, and sat up there for about 2 hours. Mum kept calling me but I just said I won't be long. Anyway, when I thought it was safe enough, I went back to the house and guess what, nothing was done and I had to do the lot. The trouble was in those days we didn't just use coffee mugs, and every time the table was set we used bread and butter plates, and cups and saucers, so there was a heap to do. I never pulled that trick again.

In the November of 1953, Dad lost his arm. He was a taxi driver when the accident happened, and Mum and I had came home from a rodeo at the Exhibition Grounds, and there were police and ambulance officers all over the place. They all came to tell us about the accident, so Mum went to the hospital to be with Dad. He was tough, and even though he had his arm ripped off, he was out of the hospital in a few weeks. Anyway, when it happened they decided to try a bit harder to stay together, so we packed up and moved to Maroochydore on the Sunshine Coast. I was 15 and met my first boyfriend who was a telegram boy, but I still couldn't go out without one of the kids chaperoning me, and I had to be home straight after the movies.

Victor was born in 1956 at Nambour Hospital and so was Tony a year later. In between Victor and Tony, Mum and Dad split up and it was really hard because we all loved Dad. The new man in Mums life said he was going to take over as head of the house and Dad had to go, and not long afer he moved in he made us all call him Dad.

After Maroochydore, we moved to Tansey where our step-father got a job on a dairy farm that had 200 milking cows. It was hard work milking all those cows every morning and night with our stepfather, but after we had been there for 6 months or so, he pissed off, leaving Mum with 10 kids on a farm, with no way of getting out. After a couple of weeks, he came back and not long after that we were sacked from the farm. So the family moved to Manyoung, and I went to work in the hotel in Goomeri, but because we lived so far away from my new job I used to catch the goods train home on my days off.

Dad as we now had to call our stepfather, was starting to pay a little more than fatherly attention to me by now, and I used to tell him if he didn't leave me alone, I would tell Mum, so he stopped. Little did I know this turned his attention to my younger sisters.

I was around 17 when we moved again to Coolangatta on

the Gold Coast, then onto Ballina. We lived in a big army tent and all the kids thought it was great because we lived near the beach, and it was like being on holidays all the time. Dad (our real father), came back and took his three sons Billy, Bart and Gary back to live with him and his girlfriend. They went for holidays for three weeks and when he brought them back, Billy didn't want to leave him. That was the last we saw of Billy, and Mum missed him so much. He went away a little boy and came back a young man, and I didn't see him again until many years after I was married.

I went to work at the Lobster Pot Hotel at Coolangatta on the Gold Coast, and always seemed to be someone's maid. I often wished I could run away but we had no other income and I was scared, and I used to believe everything Mum told me about putting the kids in a home if things got too tough. Once when we had no money (again) and Dawn was having a whinge about not being allowed to go to bingo, Mum gave her a couple of shillings to shut her up. The arsy bitch won 10 pounds, which could buy a lot in those days, so she gave it to Mum and we ended up eating well on that 10 pounds. It wasn't long after that, we moved into a house with walls and a bathroom that we could actually lock. Our stepfather had a habit of walking in and then he would pinch our breasts and it really hurt. "Oh but it was just a joke", he would say, if Mum caught him.

Anyway, we moved again to Norwell to a Sugarcane Farm and it was there that Dawn and I learnt how to cut cane. That's the hardest work we ever did. After cutting cane by hand all day in the hot sun, I remember having to soak our hands in a tub of water, still holding onto the cane knife tightly until the water helped relieve the pain of the blisters. Soaking till our broken blisters softened so we wouldn't tear our skin off when we loosened the knife from our grip.

One night Dad and Mum and Neville (my boyfriend), decided to steal a big fat sheep so we would have something to eat. Off they went about 5 miles and picked one out, and while Mum sat as lookout, Dad and Neville grabbed the sheep. It made such a racket, the farmer came out shooting his gun (lousy shot though). They got away, but it was a close shave because the car wouldn't start, and just as they got it going, the farmer showed up and they took off. Anyway, that sheep sure tasted good but we all got so sick because we ate too much freshly killed meat.

That's when Dad decided to steal some tyres to get some money so he could buy some food. He had no job and we had no money, and we had been eating sweet potatoes forever. Mum used to try and make fun of it by saying, "So, do we want them chipped, boiled or baked"? When the fat ran out, we had no choice but to have them boiled.

I think the police must have got a tip off because all of Dad's truckie mates were there and all of a sudden, there were police lights all over the place. Dad took off and the police searched the house. He hid in the swamp down the back, then when they were gone, he snuck back in the house and hid in the ceiling. He was there for some time, then we all moved to Miami on the Gold Coast.

Shane was born when I was 18 and working in the Burleigh Heads Hotel behind the bar. I was very happy there as a young handsome cop was dating me. His name was John, and I wasn't game to tell Mum about him, as Dad was on the run and still hiding out. We couldn't bring anyone home, so John used to drop me at the corner. One morning, we were sitting down to breakfast when our house was raided, and Dad jumped under the table to hide. They caught him and he was arrested and went to jail. John was one of the arresting officers and he had only been dating me so he could get closer to the house. He came and apologized to me later, but I was heartbroken.

Dad got out on bail and moved us again to Coopers Plains and it wasn't long after that, that Dawn's baby Pat was born. Not long after Dad went back to jail, but I don't remember too much about this time, because I think one tries to blot out unhappy memories. While he was in prison, Dad told a few of his buddies that we would look after them and one night three of them broke out of Wacol Prison Farm and ended up at our place. I remember one had a gun, which he was getting out a lot and going into great details about what they could do to us if we said anything. One was also a rapist, or so they said.

Anyway, Mum and I sat up all night and drank lots of tea and Mum talked a lot about giving themselves up. It must have played on their minds, because the next day, they all did give themselves up. Good Ole Mum.

When Dad finally got out of jail, we moved again to Redcliffe and then on to Scarborough, and I remember Mum and I would go out, and she always ended up with some nice gent buying drinks for us. She always managed to keep food on the table and clothes on everyone's back, but I cannot say where the money came from. Although there were no pensions or child endowment in those days, my brothers and sisters never wanted for anything and even though we were poor, we had a wonderful Mum who did everything and anything she could to keep us together. For that, I am and always will be very proud of her. It was at Scarborough, when I was at the horse races with Mum and Dad that I met my future husband, Barney. We didn't have much of a courtship and even though I was 21, I still had to take kids with me on our dates. We were married 3 months after we started dating, and 41 years later we are still blissfully happy.

CHAPTER EIGHT

My memories of my sister Dawn
(Born in 1943)

DAWN TO ME ALWAYS SEEMED a kind of a mystery, and different from the rest of us. She had short dark curly hair, and was very pretty, and although we grew up in the same household, she was a very private person. Dawn was seven years older than me and by the time I was old enough to attend school she was no doubt at a time in her life when she was interested in boys, and I can only remember bit's and pieces of our childhood years together.

Dawn often babysat for Mum, and we would always be getting on her nerves, and out of sheer frustration she would threaten to throw us in a cupboard and close the door behind us. Although this was usually enough to stop most of us from messing around, Gary would push Dawn to her limits, and If she caught him, she would throw him in the cupboard until he promised to behave himself. With both of them unwilling to give in, he was often in for a lengthy stay.

Then there was the time when I was around 8, when Mum and her sister Aunt Glady went shopping and left Dawn in charge of looking after us. She was 15 at the time, and with ten rug rats between the ages of two and fourteen running around, I'm sure she found this to be quite a challenge. But for a few pence, she was willing to go where no man had gone before; to look after all of us at the same time, and survive.

They were gone longer than Dawn had expected, and on their return Mum asked Aunty Glady if she would like a cuppa before going on her way. As she stood at the kitchen sink filling the kettle, she noticed a clay pig that she thought one of the kids had made for her, and had left on the window ledge to dry. It was so cute, right down to its button nose and curly tail. With a gleam in her eye, she gently picked it up, and proceeded to show Aunt Glady. " Look what one of the kids made for me", she proudly boasted. At almost the same time she noticed the smell. "Oh My God," she said, "this isn't clay, it's shit".

That afternoon, there was hell to pay. No one owned up, and it wasn't until my trip to Australia in December 2000, that I found out who had in fact made the shit pig. It was Dawn, dear, sweet, "butter wouldn't melt in her mouth", Dawn.

While reminiscing with my brothers and sisters on Carol's

back porch we started talking about all of the things we got up to when we were kids, and the fact that we never really knew who made the shit pig. Dawn sat there with a sheepish grin on her face and the look said it all. So, I guess she really did go where no man had previously gone.

Dawn had a baby and shortly after moved to Sydney with her husband Laurie and daughter Pat, and we didn't see her much after that, but no matter where we all lived, we always kept in touch with each other around Christmas time.

CHAPTER NINE

Dawn's own memories of her childhood.

I REMEMBER HARD TIMES WHEN ALL we had to eat was soup, which Mum just kept adding a few vegies and water to each day. We would fill ourselves up with the soup and bread, and at breakfast it was bread and milk. Mum would heat the milk and soak the bread in it and if we had any, she would sprinkle a little sugar or jam on it to sweeten it. Sometimes we would have to go and cash in bottles we found to buy things like bread, but no matter what we ate, Mum always made it taste good.

When Dad lost his arm and was still in hospital, we had some pullets that had to be killed and cleaned. Mum said she didn't know how she was going to kill and clean them for

Christmas as it had always been Dad's job, so I told her that Coral and I would do it. At the time, I was around nine or ten and had only seen Dad do this a few times, but we managed to cut their heads off with the help of a neighbor who had been watching us.

Coral held on to the pullet to keep it from moving and I swung the axe. Every time the axe came down, she would pull her hand away and let go of the pullet. and instead of chopping off its head, I would clip some other body part, and if the poor thing didn't die from loss of blood it was because it just couldn't survive without so many of its limbs. I wasn't very good with the axe and the first chop rarely killed them, so I don't know if the neighbour, who was watching from the side, helped us out of pity for us or the chickens.

Anyway, I lit a fire under the copper and when the water was boiling I dipped them in like I had seen Dad do many times before. Before putting them in the boiling water, I cut their bums off, and put my hand in and pulled out all the insides; at least I thought I did. Everyone had a pullet each for dinner, but it wasn't until they started eating that it was discovered that I had left their feedbags in the stomachs. I think they call it the gullets, but anyway, I didn't feel too proud that I had left the innens in them.

Around the age of seven to ten, I was always sick, and whenever my birthday would arrive Mum would give me a big party and all of the adults would stand around and cry. I didn't know but at the time they thought I was going to die. I now look back and think, I bet you kids used to think "why the hell did I get special treatment?". Anyway, I ended up spending a lot of time in hospital and had my lung taken out, and it left a big scar on my back.

I remember when Aunty Glady's mob and our lot got together, and one year Mum was in hospital around the time you were born Wendy, and I was getting looked after by the O'Leary's (Aunty Glady's mob). I saw Uncle Matt put all this black stuff on his meat pie, so I did the same. Little did I realize that it was hot Black Sauce and Uncle Matt made me eat the whole lot. Boy, I never did that ever again.

Coral and I always knew when Mum was pregnant. She had a real craving for Caramello chocolate bars, and as soon as we saw them in the fridge, we knew. She couldn't stand them any other time but we had Caramello bars a lot, because she was always pregnant.

When we lived on the farm at Gumdale, we had a pet duck called Donald. He was a great pet and would come under the kitchen table and we would give him our food scraps. One Christmas, we went to Nana Clarke's place for Christmas dinner, and as we all sat around the table she came out of the kitchen and said, "Guess what you're eating". It was Donald and just about everyone pushed their dinner away. She was really nasty and got great joy at seeing us upset about Donald.

I remember when I was ten, Mum used to let me go to the pictures on a Saturday afternoon with Coral so I could watch that she didn't get into mischief. Coral was thirteen and I was her chaperone and at the time she used to sit in the back of the pictures with the boys. They would give me money to get rid of me, and I would go down to the counter and stuff myself on OKAY bars and Lollies and when I ran out, I would go back, and if they wanted to get rid of me again, they would have to give me more money. I had a real racket going and Mum would ask, had Coral behaved herself and I would say yes.

With so many of us to get ready, everywhere we went, Mum was always prepared to leave early. She hated turning up late anywhere we went, so we would all be dressed and ready to go well before time. On the other hand, when we went to Mum's sister Aunty Glady's place, who also had 12 kids she was completely the opposite to Mum and would just be setting her hair as we arrived to go out.

When I was thirteen, I put my age up to get a job as we needed the money. Coral and I never got to keep our wages (none). Our clothes were second hand most of the time, but I think we always looked ok. Mum was always strict, but I suppose she had to be, and we all had our jobs to do around the house, and boy, we had to do them or else we got a good wallop. Mum always made our home nice, even when she didn't have much. I remember when long dining room tables came into fashion and Mum cut our table up the middle and then discovered she had to have two extra legs for the middle. We ended up with this long table that had a dip in the middle because the two legs we found were short. It had its good points though, and when someone would say "pass the jam", all you had to do was give it a slight touch and away it would go, sliding up the table.

It was around this time that kitchen cupboards on the wall above the counter tops became a fashion, so Mum cut her larger cupboard in half and nailed one half on the wall with two large nails. She asked me to set the table one day and as I was getting the knifes and forks out, the cupboard on the wall fell on me and knocked me out. When I came to, all I could hear was Mum saying that I had broken all of her mother's plates. I felt pretty lousy but it wasn't my fault.

I remember when I was around eleven, living at Maroochydore, Mum would let me stay home from school if I did some of the work. I used to hang the washing on my knees as I didn't want to be seen by my teacher who used to walk past our house on her way to school.

That was around the time Mum and Dad split up, and our step father came on the scene. I remember there was a big fight and I went and hid in the outside toilet.

CHAPTER TEN

My memories of my sister Jacqueline
(Born in 1945)

J ACQUELINE WAS BORN, AND DIED before I ever came along, and the only recollection I have of her, are those passed on to me by my older siblings and mother. From what I hear, she was a sweet little thing, however when she was born, she had a condition called Hemolytic Anemia of the newborn, which affects the white blood cells.

Back in 1945, the delivery of a baby was a rather laborious experience which necessitated both mother and baby spending two weeks or more in hospital recuperating.

Within the first eleven weeks of her birth, Jacqueline had ten blood transfusions, however fifty five years ago a transfusion wasn't the simple procedure it is today. With each one requiring a slit in the arm big enough to warrant two stitches to close it after the process, she spent a lot of time in hospital. After the transfusions, Mum said Jacqueline improved enough to go home, and although she was sick in the beginning she recovered and was a joy to her family until her sudden death in 1947.

Even though Jacqueline died over 55 years ago, whenever we pass the funeral home where she was buried it brings a tear to Mum's eyes. I wonder how Jacqueline would have influenced our lives, had we been blessed with more time with her.

CHAPTER ELEVEN

My memories of my oldest brother William (Billy)
(Born in 1946)

THE FIRST BOY TO BE BORN, Billy was the apple of our
father's eye I'm sure. Our parents separated when he
was 10, and I remember this day as if it was yesterday;
all of us lined up like Browns Cows, having to decide which
side of the line we wanted to go.

It was during this time that we lived in a huge tent and
we were rounded up for a "big important meeting". Mum and
Dad had parted a short time earlier, and Dad came back to see
if any of us wanted to be with him, and we were told to decide
there and then which parent we wanted to be with.

I don't know why the others chose Mum, but I remember

thinking at the time, "where would I spend the night if I went with Dad?". It wasn't that I loved Dad any more than I did Mum, but at the age of 5 I was more concerned about being with my brothers and sisters, and where I would lay my head. After all, even though we lived in a tent, it had all the comforts of home.

I remember when everyone had finished choosing who they wanted to be with, no one stood beside Dad, and Billy stepped forward and went to his side, but I have a feeling it was more for the need to comfort Dad than not to be with us. Dad wanted to take the two youngest boys as well as Billy, so Barton and Gary went with him as well. Off they went with him and the rest of us stayed with Mum. A couple of weeks after they left, Dad returned Gary and Bart, because he couldn't handle them, and that was the last we saw of Billy for nearly ten years.

When he came back into our lives, we lived on Bribie Island, a small island just off the Queensland Coast. Close enough to the mainland to be considered part of it, Bribie had that small town feeling about it and was the kind of place where everyone knew everyone else's business. I was 15 at the time and working in the local pub, and when Billy came back no one on Bribie knew of him; so I wasn't surprised when word got out that I had a new boyfriend, and he wasn't one of the locals.

It was great to have Billy back in our lives again, and a few years after he returned he became a successful brickie with several crews of men working under him. He was constantly working and on the go, and he was happily married with two beautiful children, David and Lisa.

Billy had been suffering from headaches for about 6 weeks, but his male ego pride got the better of him and instead of going to the doctor, he started popping across the counter headache pills. One day, at the age of 35 while he was out water-skiing with his wife Wendy, he had an accident.

As soon as he took his hands off the skiing rope and grabbed his head, Wendy (who was a nurse at the time), knew something was wrong . He was rushed to hospital, where they discovered that he'd had a brain hemorrhage, and he spent several weeks in the intensive care unit.

It wasn't until six weeks after the accident, that he was moved from the IT unit to an open ward and we were able to visit him. Mum, my sisters and I went up to the hospital in the one car all very excited and a little anxious, as we had been warned not to expect him to remember us.

As we all sat around his bed, we talked about old times, reminiscing and trying to refresh his memory. Each of us spent some time alone with him, we held his hand, and stroking his hair we told him how much we loved him. When it was time to leave, we all gave him a big kiss and cuddle, but it wasn't until we got outside the hospital doors, that we all looked at each other and divulged that Billy had actually given all of us including Mum, a big toungy.

Afterwards, it was explained to us that Billy's brain had

been damaged, and he didn't recognized that doing such a thing with your sisters and mother was morally objectionable, and against normal family values. He also had little recollection of the past, but developed a real knack of having us believe he did. I have a feeling this was to get us off his back more than anything else.

Because of Billy's accident and his inability to recognize right from wrong, his marriage soon fell apart and for many years, he drifted between half-way houses, and living in parks with other street people on welfare. His fortnightly welfare cheque was quickly used up on alcohol, and until the next cheque arrived he survived on handouts and help from shelters.

My eldest sister Coral and her husband Barney, lived in Redland Bay which is a hop, skip and jump from Brisbane and the parks that Billy frequented. Sometimes, she wouldn't see him for months then all of a sudden, out of the blue, he would show up without a word on her doorstep. She would of course welcome him with open arms, and after they chinwaged for a few hours, he would disappear just as casually as he arrived.During these visits, Billy would often put Coral's husband's clothes on, and make out that he had leant them to Barney years earlier, and that he was now taking them back. I recall Coral telling me of a time when Billy came to her house after several months, and he stayed for a couple of days. As he was leaving he walked out wearing Barney's good safari suite and Coral was fuming. She would normally let him get away with whatever he was wearing, but not this time, They got into a big argument, and finally Billy gave in, declared that "Barney could have his bloody suite back, even though it was his"; he took it off, and proceeded to walk out of the house, naked. Coral and Barney finally gave in and let him have it. The suit that is.

On the odd occasion Billy would stay for the whole weekend at Coral and Barney's, but as the rest of us had small children and he had a tendency not be to trusted around them, Coral kept our whereabouts from him for as long as she could. Christmas cards from us to him never had the return address on them, but I'm sure Coral had a good reason for this whenever he questioned it.

I do recall, a period of time not long after his accident and before he became dependant on drugs and booze when he would pay us the occasional visit on the Gold Coast (an hour's drive from Coral's place). This was during the early stages of his addiction and he would often go to the pub at Broadbeach, not far from where we lived, and get so drunk that he couldn't remember where he had parked his car. He would call the police and report it missing, but of course every time he did this he wasn't capable of driving anyway, and as the police were familiar with his antics, they would find his car for him, and make sure it was locked, before dropping him off at our house.

One of my sisters lived about 20 kilometers from our place on the Coast, in a small town called Nerang, and she began getting phone calls from a stranger. They seemed innocent enough in the beginning and as they were infrequent she thought that perhaps they were school kids playing a prank on her. She brushed them off as childish behavior, but as time went by, the caller became more vulgar and the loose chit chat took a turn to down right obscenity; with this Teresa called the police and a trace was put on her phone.

After monitoring the caller for the next few days, the police tracked him down to a local caravan park. It was the same park that Billy resided in, and we found out that he had been making the calls, however, because he was disguising his voice Teresa didn't realize it was him.

Billy became addicted to cheap wines, spirits and drugs, and died in an old derelict building on the Gold Coast after it caught fire in 1996. He was 50 years old.

Three bodies were discovered in the ashes, however they were unrecognizable, and it wasn't until a few days after the fire, when Coral was watching the news on TV, that she recognized a ring that had been recovered from the ashes. It was a ring that Billy always wore, and that she had given him years earlier. She wasn't too concerned that she hadn't seen Billy, as he tended to be a bit of a loner. That was until the fire, and the day she saw his ring.

Many years before his death, Billy's daughter Melissa became a nun and teacher and although she never got to know her father as she was growing up, she was able to spend some time with him just before he died. After finding out which park he frequented, she sat down beside him, and even though he didn't recognize her, they struck up a conversation. Every day for a week, she would go to the park and find him sitting on the same bench.

They talked but she soon noticed that he became restless when the afternoon approached. She could see that he relied on liquor to get him through the rest of the day, so she would plan her visits with him for the mornings. Before she went back to New Zealand, she revealed to him that she was in fact his daughter.

He was overjoyed with excitement and told Coral about Melissa's visit. Coral of course listened to him, but because of his tendency to fantasize, deep down she thought he was just pulling her leg. She found out he was telling the truth on the day of his funeral when she was talking to Melissa.

I do miss the times he isn't with us, and the memories this would have created.

CHAPTER TWELVE

My memories of my sister Teresa
(Born in 1947)

TERESA TO ME IS OUR GUARDIAN ANGEL. Oh, don't get me wrong, she's no saint; but oh, could she calm the waters during the rough times. She was always sweet and kind and never had a bad thing to say about anyone, and to this day, she is a tower of strength and I admire her tremendously.

I always thought she had a kind of angelic look about her and wasn't surprised to hear that she was thinking of joining a nunnery. Not long after this thought crossed her mind however, and contrary to a nun's beliefs, she entered and made it into the finals in the Miss Queensland Surf Girl competition. She always seemed so quiet and shy, so I was surprised to see her go in such a large beauty pageant. She looked beautiful and made it into the top ten, and I thought she was a real trooper to get up in front of all of those people.

On the day of the bathing suit competition, the finalists sat on stage, with each of them being asked to step up to the podium for a brief conversation with the compare. As Teresa waited her turn, Mum noticed her posture wasn't very lady-like. There she was, sitting up on stage, the only one of the 10 finalists with her legs uncrossed and more concerned about what she was going to say than how she looked. Mum sent Shane up to the stage to discretely tell Teresa to "close her legs" and as hard as he tired to pass on Mum's message he couldn't. Several times Teresa tried to hear what he was saying, but she couldn't hear him. Shane, who was only 5 at the time, was so frustrated, he yelled at the top of his lungs, "Mum said, close your legs and sit up properly". Everyone looked at her and she was so embarrassed she turned beet red.

There was a time when three of us (Teresa, Desley and myself), shared an 8 feet x 10 feet bedroom with two double decker beds in it and we would often share stories, makeup, and clothes. When she was around 16 she developed shingles, which is a nerve rash with an irritating itch that drove her crazy every waking moment. For several weeks, it kept her awake all night and Desley and I would take turns and sit beside her for what seemed like hours scratching the itch, trying to make it go away. We had heard that if the rash went from one side of the body around to the other and eventually joined, she would die, so Desley and I sat scratching, not knowing any better. It eventually healed, and she made a full recovery.

It was when we moved to Pierces Dairy Farm that Teresa saw her first goat shit, and she couldn't believe it. All of these watermelon seeds lying around everywhere, and with spring just around the corner, she was sure to have a bumper crop. She was determined to keep it a secret from Mum and Dad and started collecting the seeds to plant, and she soon had herself a small veggie garden. It seemed that no matter how much love and care, watering and sunshine she devoted to it, nothing happened, and it wasn't until a few weeks later that she was told that fertilizer isn't going to help anything grow, unless there's something else in the ground with it.

The goat that left all the droppings in our yard, had been on loan from a neighbouring farm and they would often bring it over to keep the grass down around the house. When the neighbors sold their property they gave the goat to us, so now we had our own goat. Dad fenced the back yard to keep it in but as the dunny was in the same yard you had to sprint past the goat to get to it in one piece. I guess this is what they call the runs!

One day, Teresa went missing but no one thought to check the dunny. The goat had her trapped in it and every time she peeked through one of the holes in the walls, there it was, looking back at her. By the time they found her, she was pretty distraught, and after that it took ages for her to get the courage to go to the toilet by herself.

She was really popular with the boys, and while in her mid teens she dated a Navy guy and at one stage, they talked of marriage. Whenever he was on leave, he would visit her, and for weeks before she would be so excited Desley and I couldn't stand it. Teresa was wrapped up in John and devoted most of her spare time writing love letters and reading his, and I remember every letter she sent was sealed with a kiss. She would put fresh lipstick on and practice to get it just right, and then she would plant a big kiss on the page before gently folding it and sealing it in an envelope.

One day, while his ship was on a peace time training mission just off the Australian coast, there was in a terrible accident. At three o'clock in the morning, as most of the sailors lay sleeping, another Navy war ship collided with his and tore a huge hole in the sleeping quarters. As news of the accident was flashed on every newspaper and TV Australia wide, Teresa's spirit sunk to an all time low, and it wasn't until three days after the accident that John's death was confirmed.

She was on her way to work when word came through, and Mum sent Desley, Gary and I after her to let her know. To this day I can still see her walking under the trees through the park as we ran after her yelling out that John was dead. We were only kids at the time, and we didn't think about how she was feeling, but in retrospect, I wish we had been more considerate and broken the news to her more gently. How could such an horrific accident invade their young lives as they lay sleeping and dreaming about the loved ones they would soon be seeing, unaware that their lives would be in danger so close to home.

Teresa eventually fell in love and married a local Bribie Island guy. Although Arthur was a shy quiet guy, he was popular with the girls and was a member of the local surf club, Teresa would often point him out to me whenever we went down the beach, so I wasn't surprised when they started dating, and eventually married. They had three beautiful sons, John, Shawn and Darryl.

A few years after Teresa and Arthur married, she moved to the Gold Coast not far from where I lived. During the Summer of 1976 when it was extremely hot and muggy, we decided to take the kids to the local swimming hole, so we packed a picnic lunch and cordial, planning on making a day of it. Both of us had three boys, and as Desley had to go to work that particular

Saturday we were also looking after her kids. The nieces and nephews were all around the same age and they all got on extremely well, so everyone was excited and looking forward to the day.

The beach we went too had plenty of shady areas in the park, and the calm waters allayed parents fears of a wave knocking the little ones over, but little did we realize as we went about our day, that there were other hidden dangers lurking.

We had been down at the beach for quite some time, taking turns at holding each of the kids by their arms and legs and tossing them into the water; just as our parents did with us when we were kids. As each of them had a go they would come up splattering and go to the back of the line to wait their next turn, but after doing this for quite some time, when it came to Shawn's turn, he was no where to be seen.

Our immediate thought was that he had wondered off into the park and everyone started calling out his name, but after a few minutes of looking Teresa's motherly instincts kicked in and she realized that he hadn't wandered off, but even worse, had been abducted or was still in the water. We tried everything and looked everywhere in a desperate attempt to find him, and although Shawn was 9 and only a year younger than my oldest son Jason and his cousin Alan, they knew he was an epileptic and he couldn't swim. Both of them started diving in the water in a last ditch effort to find him.

Everyone in the park, including strangers started looking for him, but by late afternoon he was still nowhere to be seen. While Teresa remained at the park with the search party a police officer drove me to Arthur's job where he worked as a bricklayer, but as we pulled up to his work place I froze and couldn't get out of the car. The police officer, who was obviously experienced at dealing with these types of situations, was able to convince me to stay positive and I told Arthur what had happened; at the time I'm sure he firmly believed that Shawn had done what he had done many time before, and had simply wandered off.

As we didn't live far from the park, I took Teresa and the other kids home while Arthur stayed with the search party, however, as we drove away the police boat had just pulled up and was about to drop the grappling hooks over the side. On seeing this the thought of her baby still in the water was too much for Teresa and she just lost it. At one stage as the car was still moving, I thought she was going to jump out, so I held on to her with all my might. Up until then, there was still hope, but the boat and grappling hooks made Teresa think of the other possibility, that Shawn had drowned, and this was simply too much for her to bear.

When I got her home, she sat on the back steps of the house smoking one cigarette after another, and although she knew he was under the water, her only concern at that time was that he didn't have a sweater on, and he would be cold. I realize now that she was in a great deal of shock, but 25 years ago, it was up to family to support each other through such a tragedy. If a child went missing today there would be grief councilors and church groups helping out.

They found Shawn's body at 9am the following morning, only about 6 feet from where we were playing with him the day before. He had waded into one of the dips created by the incoming and outgoing tide, and even though it was only a small hole, it was deep enough for him not to be able to touch bottom. They told Teresa he had a smile on his face, and although this comforted her, it was no compensation for his loss.

Shawn was a very special little boy, who touched everyone's lives. He suffered from epilepsy, sometimes having as many as 60 convulsions a day, but he never once let his disability affect his good nature. He loved opening envelopes, and he and I would have battles whenever he got to the letterbox before I did. By the time I got the mail, he had opened it and in the excitement of doing so, practically destroyed the entire contents. If only he were here now, I would gladly mail a dozen to him every day, just to see the pure joy of receiving them on his face.

On September 13, 2002, I took my yearly trip back to Australia feeling confident that this time there would be no family tragedy or sorrow, and apart from the usual ailments Mum was experiencing, everyone seemed in good health and looking forward to catching up. Unbeknown to me, however, Teresa had been having tests done for what she thought was fluid retention and the occasional stomach pain, and a few days before I was due to fly back to Canada her doctor called her in to go over the results.

It wasn't good news and she was immediately scheduled in to see a specialist, and a barrage of tests were organized. I put my trip back to Canada off for another week and went with her to see the specialist who informed her that she had a 20 x 9cm growth in her stomach and regardless of the results of future tests, it had to be removed. Even in light of such news Teresa's sense of humor shone through, and she asked the doctor if it had arms and legs, and that perhaps it was that daughter she had always wanted. She even named it Little Tess after herself.

Before our youngest sister Carol passed away from her battle with cancer in May 2001, Teresa took 4 months off work to look after her. Many times she showed symptoms of fatigue herself, but any ailments she experienced seemed trivial compared to what Carol was going through so she brushed it off to deal with at a later date. It's not unusual for a care giver to neglect themselves when caring for a loved one.

Just before Carol passed away she whispered in Teresa's ear that she wished she could take her with her, so the running joke for the first few days after Teresa got the news about her own cancer, was that Carol was determined to get her up there, the bitch!

When does it end; maybe the end is just the beginning, and this is just a prelude of what life is really about.

CHAPTER THIRTEEN

Teresa's memories of her childhood

I RECALL WE GOT OUR FIRST SURFBOARD when I was about 13 or 14 and we lived on Bribie Island. We all chipped in for this old 9 ft 10 inch Bolster Wood Surfboard, and boy did we have fun on it. One of us could carry it to the beach, but because it had so many dings in it after being in the water all day, it got so water logged, it took four of us to carry it back home.

Everyone would shoot off home after a day in the surf, and the last one out of the water would have to drag this huge water logged board up the beach to our house. Fortunately we only lived a short distance from the beach but the drag marks in the sand was a dead set giveaway that one of the Clarke girls had been abandoned and left to get the thing home. Anyway, we all thought we were pretty cool as we were the only girls around at the time to ride a surfboard.

I worked in a local hamburger shop when we lived on Bribie, and at the time a peeping tom was going around perving on the local girls. The shop owner Mr. Warner caught him in the act one day, getting his jollies off while spying on me through the back fence. It wasn't so funny at the time, but when I look back I get a good laugh at seeing old Mr. Warner coming back into the shop after confronting "Tom" with hamburger all over his hair and face.

Mum always tried to keep up with our demands for the latest in fashions, and even though it was always hand me downs or second hand shops, we always looked good. The boys thought so too, as we were never short of dates, but I remember I only ever wanted to be friends with all my boy friends, and as soon as the pressure was on, I would be off.

I loved being around my brothers and sisters and as each one left home, I missed them terribly. When Coral left home and we didn't see her for years, it took me a long time to get over it. I would wake up at night crying under my pillow for her. It might have been only a few days, but to a little girl it was forever. I missed her so much, but the one I missed the most was Dawn. That sounds strange to me because I was always a little frightened of her, but when she left I felt lost as she was my security, like a Mum whenever Mum was away, and I'll always love her for that. I was sad also, because our stepfather put more pressure on me.

I remember too living in a big tent, but I think it started out as a holiday, and things got out of hand. That was about the time Billy was taken away from us and as I was only young, in my mind, he was taken. I realized later that he went to live with our Dad when he and Mum separated.

Another time, when we lived in Scarborough, Mum, Aunty Glady, and a few of us kids, were walking along the beach near the old Scarborough Pier. There was this piercing scream coming from the jetty where you (Wendy) and Bart, and some other kids were swimming. You had jumped off the pier right in the middle of a big slimy brown sea stinger called a Portuguese Man-O-War.

Mum just jumped in and I have never see her swim so fast. I remember thinking how fast she could swim and how brave she was. Bart also got stung under the arms trying to help you, but you got the full blunt of it and we nearly lost you. It took weeks for you to get over it. (Good on ya Mum)

At sixteen, I came second in the Miss Bribie Island pageant, and went on to represent the Bribie Surf Club in the Miss Queensland Surf Girl pageant. There were about 80 girls in it, and I was one of the top ten to get into the finals. I didn't win, and although Mum and the other family members encouraged me to go in it, originally I didn't want to. You see, they saw things in me I couldn't, but I'm glad I did it now, because of the experience. It gave me a lot more confidence in myself, and believe it or not, I was very shy and didn't like myself back then. I think that was because of what Dad did in our younger days. I couldn't stand him looking at me when I was in my togs or shorts, and would always keep myself covered whenever he was around as he liked making crude remarks.

He was sent to Wacol Prison for stealing, when I was around 10 years old, and we lived in Bradman Street, in Coopers Plains. I would spend most Sundays catching two trains to the prison, to take him his parcel of goodies. I would drop them off at the prison office, and then catch the trains back home, but I always thought that was the place where he worked. I didn't mind going so much, as I had my bag of lollies to keep to myself, but sometimes you would come with me Wendy, but not too often because you didn't like it. Anyway, by the time I got home, I was high from all that sugar and I really didn't mind, it was fun and made me feel all grown up.

When Shane was around 9 years old, he said to Mum he was becoming a man because he had two black hairs on one toe and one hair on the other. He was always a very curious little boy and at one stage he asked Mum if ants in China had slant eyes. I remember when I was very young and staying at Nana Clark's place and her and Aunt Lilly would take me to the corner store and buy ice-blocks. I still get home sick whenever I go anywhere near that place, and pass that old store. They were the good old days.

Barton was named after our Grandfather Barton. He was always hurting himself and I remember when he was around two years old he broke his two collar bones, one after the other, and at age five or six he had both of his legs broken. He copped a lot about his name from everyone, and us kids even made up a poem about it, and boy did he get mad when we sang it. Around 15 he changed his name to Barney, and I can see why.

Barton, Barton
Fell down farting.
Got up stinking
Run away winking.

When Coral was around 14, she used to ride our horse name Girlie to the shop. Girlie had a foal, and one day when Coral was riding her, our brother Billy who was around 7 at the time was running beside them. Next thing the foal got out and chased after them, and it ran straight over the top of Billy and he had broken bones and skin ripped off him from head to toe.

At the age of 9 or 10, Carol had her first ride on an old Clydesdale horse. Dad put her on the back of it and just as he did, the thing took off with Mum running behind yelling out "get her off, it will kill her". Dad always believed that the best way to learn anything was to just do it, and to teach Coral and Dawn to swim, he just threw them in the deep end and told Mum to watch them, and sure enough, they swam.

Note: During our youngest sister Carol's fight with cancer, with her bosses blessing, Teresa took her long service leave from where she worked as a matron at a private school in Southport. She wrote the following section when her three months leave was nearly up; and again shortly after Carol passed away on May 11, 2001.

Just another short letter with news that I got my airline

ticket to go back home today after spending three months looking after Carol. I leave on the 19 May and boy it's going to be very hard. I just hope I'm around when the time comes for Carol to go on ahead. It's hard watching our sister die, but if there's anything good that has come out of this, it is the fact that it has made me a stronger person and I love every bit of life, and I think we are lucky.

I had always promised Carol that I would always be around for her, and that she would never be alone when the time came, so when they got the bad news that her time was near, Steve called me as soon as they found out. Carol only had a few weeks to live and I thought I would be prepared for it, but when I received the call it was such a shock.

I'm feeling sad tonight because it's hard watching someone you love die and everyday thinking that it will be her last. She is having trouble breathing and the doctor has put her on Ventalair, along with a combination of 15 different drugs, all to improve the quality of her life, but she is still in a lot of pain and is on such a high, I wonder if it's all worth it for her?

I wish I could take some of it for her, and I'm glad I could look after her because she would have been in hospital most of the time, and her wish was to come home to die. The hospital said they wouldn't let her out if someone couldn't spend 24 hours a day with her. I have a chart to follow for her medication that has to be filled in every day for the hospital, and there's so much to do. I had seen her go through hell and she was always so brave and strong, I admired her so much and looked up to her, I think the sad thing about this, is that we all took it for granted that Carol would always be around, I think it was because she was always so positive which reflected on us, she always bounced back no matter how ill she was and I'm just not ready for this.

I remember her telling me when she first got cancer, "I wont let this get hold of me, I'll beat it," that was Carol, Mrs. Positive. It's just as well she was like that because she gave me the best times of my life. We had lots of fun times, some sad but mostly good.

Most of the family spent her last Xmas with her, that was her wish to have all her family with her and what a day it was, we all made sure it was the best. Most of us still didn't believe she was dying and thought she would still beat it. But not this time, and as I was nearing the end of my three months long service which was due to end on May 19, I decided to go back early to tell my boss at TSS that I wouldn't be back until it was all over. I couldn't leave Carol now and they were very supportive and understood and I went back to look after her so she could spend her last few weeks in her new home, and not in hospital. I spent every minute with her right to the end.

I can't explain how I felt, but I do remember her last week in hospital. I kept thinking I was the only one in this and it wasn't really happening, it was a dream and I would wake up and she would be sitting up in bed. But that wasn't the case, because every day she just got worse. I wished one of my brothers or sisters would walk in, just so I could talk to someone about how I was feeling. I couldn't talk to Steve or the kids; they were having a hard enough time watching their mother and partner die. Sometimes, I hated everyone and felt I was being punished in some way. Don't get me wrong I loved looking after Carol; it just got harder towards the end just watching her go like this. Seeing her fade away to a shadow and knowing her body was shutting down but her mind was still so alert.

She became a little aggressive towards the end and told Steve, the kids and me that she only wanted us around her. She didn't want anyone else seeing her like this, and only wanted the ones who had been with her everyday from the start. She was worried about all the family members and especially Mum, and didn't want her or anyone else to see how she was changing.

A few of the family members found the fact that they couldn't see her again hard to accept, and I think some of them thought it was my fault. They thought that all I had to do was leave the room and let them in, but that wasn't the case because her wish was to not let anyone else see her the way she was. Steve and I agreed to carry out her wish but no one understood and I felt like I lost more than one family member at this time

The doctors increased Carol's morphine to induce sleep but she told me she wanted to say goodbye to Mum before it was too late. I know if I was Mum I would have wanted to be there with her; to hold them for the last time in my arms and say good bye. I phoned Mum so Carol could talk to her; and I felt so helpless, all I could think of was my poor Mum and my poor Carol. I just sat outside in the hallway and cried my heart out, I have never prayed so much in my life.

Steve stayed with Carol that last week at the hospital, and I stayed just up from them in another room. I remember not being able to sleep and I would go down and just sit in the dark and hold her hand. I wanted to make it easy for her and I didn't want to leave, in case she went while I was away some place.

Steve went home on the Thursday night with Mel and her husband Shane, but I had a feeling Carol was waiting for them to go because she went down hill fast after they left. Friday morning her breathing changed and I just held her and said "you have to let go sweetheart, its time to go and its OK, we'll see you soon in the blink of an eye". I just wanted to go with her, and I felt so alone, I was numb. I now know you can never prepare yourself for something like this.

By 8.30am we knew it was nearly time, and the hospital rang Steve and the kids to come to the hospital while I stayed with Carol. I kept telling her "I love you Carol", and I talked to her, and I said, "Remember the promise we made to one another, when you get up there you will be a Mum to Shawn and I'll be a Mum to your kids until we all meet again". I was praying and hoping that one of the family would walk in.

This may sound strange but I felt our deceased brother Gary's presence in the room, then the strangest thing happened.

Just as Carol was taking her last breath, Gary's wife's arms went around me. Gay had walked into the room just as Carol was going, and I remember her handing me a tissue and wiping the tears from the corner of Carol's eyes. It is something I will always remember, it was such a special moment because Carol knew she was going. She died on Friday, May 11th at 10 am, but Steve and the kids didn't get a chance to hold her before she went. I felt sad, anger, relief and guilt all at the same time, and didn't want to talk to anybody.

Before Carol passed away, we talked about her funeral, and went over everything she wanted for that day. She wanted to wear her wedding dress and was so worried that the funeral home would put too much makeup on her and have her looking like a clown, so I made a promise that I would do it for her.

The afternoon before the funeral, I went down to the funeral home and I was so scared that I wouldn't be able to handle seeing her, but when I got there they assured me that she was fine. I remember looking down at her and thinking how beautiful and at peace she looked. She had such a natural beauty, and her skin was so clear, she didn't need any makeup, so I put just a little on her, and with her wedding dress, she looked like a doll.

I sat and talked to her for a while and told her how proud I was of her and thanked her for being my sister and giving me so many great times. I know she was with all of us on that day and everyday after. Be in peace our sweet Carol we love you.

Remember "See you soon in the blink of an eye".

CHAPTER FOURTEEN

My memories of my brother Barton
(Born in 1949)

BART WAS BORN ONE YEAR AND one day before me, so we often celebrated our birthdays together. When we were small we looked so much alike people thought we were twins; that is until his male hormones kicked in and he shot up and out.

During Bart's sixteen and my fifteenth birthday, Mum and Dad put on a beach party. At that time we were well into surfing and the opposite sex, and many of the Bribie kids around our age attended. We were at an age and time when the Gidget surfing movies were all a rage, and the beach party Mum put on could have come straight from one of the Gidget sets.

Surfboards stood up everywhere, and the music of the

Beach Boys, Bobby Darren and Petula Clarke could be heard around the sand dunes. Everyone sat around a roaring beach fire eating hot dogs and fruit salad out of half pineapples, and Mum and Dad hung around until they became embarrassing; but as soon as they left we paired off and started playing spin the bottle.

Although Bart was a great looking guy and was very popular with the girls, he was forever dribbling and I was always telling him to wipe his mouth. Thank god he remembered to do it when the bottle started spinning.

He loved animals and at one time he had raised several ducklings as pets. He didn't realize at the time that Mum and Dad had raised them to make some money and they had already been sold, and Bart was just fattening them up for the neighbors. On the day Dad wanted to hand them over to the neighbours, Mum had taken us out, but it wasn't until our return that we realized why. We arrived back too early and there, strung out along the clothesline were Bart's pet ducks, all headless with blood still dripping from their cut throats.

We were all so upset and of course Dad wouldn't let us bury the bodies, so we buried the heads with the rosary beads that we had used for the other burials. The next morning when we visited the grave all that remained was a deep hole from where the wild dogs had dug up the remains during the night, and again the rosary beads were left behind.

While living on the dairy farm, we looked after a menagerie of animals for the owners, and one day one of the female pigs rolled over onto her piglets. One of them was badly injured, and Bart nursed her for several weeks, and kept her beside the kitchen stove fueled by the wood fire to keep her warm. Although she looked like she was coming around she developed pneumonia and died. After a rather long service and a few religious words over her small frame we buried her with the rosary beads on the hill behind the house. Too bad the dingo's didn't have the same moral values, but at least we got our rosary beads back.

Bart was fun to hang around with. His friends all rode surfboards and were the perfect age for my younger sister Desley and I. We were always hanging around them, but of course we pretended we were more interested in surfing, but spent most of our time ogling and sizing them up. Desley, Teresa and I all rode boards during our early teen years, and as all of Bart's friends belonged to the local surf club, it wasn't unusual to see us down at the beach at six in the morning on the weekend. He loved sports, especially swimming and because of his natural ability in this event he represented many of the schools we attended. When he was around 14 he moved away from home and boarded at a catholic school for boys called De La Sel College and he joined their swimming team. He was also a very strong surf swimmer and took part in many Life Saving Carnivals.

For most of his teenage years he was a member of Surf Lifesaving Clubs, and throughout his life and even to this day he has played a part in many rescues. At the age of 55, Bart still rides his big Mal surfboard.

*The following is an excerpt taken from The West Australian Motoring magazine published December 1999.

Perth truck driver Barton Clarke, did not think twice when he spotted a partly submerged car in a swollen river earlier this year. He strode into a swollen river to pull a young girl and her mother from a vehicle that was dangerously close to being swept farther downstream. The Bibra Lake driver was delivering cars to Karratha when he noticed the car and without hesitation he pulled his rig up and went to the rescue.

By the time he had gotten the little girl out, another driver stopped to help and they not only got everyone out, but also winched the car back to the road and worked on the engine until they got it started. Bart then headed off, thinking that was the last he would hear of the rescue. However, somebody at the scene noted a telephone number on the back of his truck and rang Finemores, the company he works for.

Finemores operations Manager, Mr Hilston later nominated Bart for the award, but it wasn't the first rescue for the unassuming Bart, a former lifesaver who is still an avid surfer. Some time ago, he helped pull several people from a submerged four wheel drive. A humble Bart just said, "Most people would do the same thing if somebody is in danger, and to me it wasn't a big deal". He said, that was the worse accident he had come across but they got everyone out, but he had nightmares after that one.

Bart believes that truckies are duty-bound to keep an eye out for motorists, especially tourists in the north, as many have no idea of how harsh the region could be and how far it is between roadhouses.

CHAPTER FIFTEEN

Bart's memories of his childhood.

Bart was never one for writing, so the following are his memories (word for word), captured on a tape recorder that he carried around with him while out trucking.

G IDDAY SIS, HOW'S IT GOING? I was suppose to try and remember some of the things in my life for your story, but I don't remember much. The first thing I remember is laying in a cot watching Mum hang out the clothes on the clothes line in a back yard. I don't know how old I was but I know she always worked hard for us and she was out there hanging the clothes.

The next thing I remembered was me 5th birthday, I was given a little toy gun and I went across the road to a beach where we were playing cowboys and that and me gun was lost. I came home and got a hiding because it cost a lot of money for the gun and I don't think Dad was working at the time.

Me first day at school was a beauty. I was playing with some kids, they were a few years older than me and I thought I could keep up with them and play the game with them called Bedlam. There were two teams and one team caught the other team and put'em in a ring, and when you got out, you had to run through the ring to get your friends out. Most of the guys in my team were in the ring at the time, and I thought me being the last one, that I was pretty quick because they hadn't caught me yet, but actually I wasn't.

I tried to run through the ring and this kid saw me coming and he decided he was going to grab me, but instead of grabbing me, he jumped on top of me, and the next thing I remember I was lying in Nambour Hospital with plaster from me chest down to me left ankle. I was put into an adult ward but I didn't like it there much so I kicked up a bit of a stink for quite a while, so they decided to put me out onto the verandah.

It wasn't a bad idea actually, because I had the whole verandah for meself. I could watch people come and go, and I could look down the car park and see people pulling up, and I used to look forward to seeing Mum and Dad visiting, but unfortunately they decided they were going to move onto a farm and they told me they were going to move closer to the hospital but they didn't, they moved further away and I only got to see them once just before I was due to come out.

I remember walking around with one leg stuck out side-
ways swinging it all in plaster and walking around like a duck,
and I used to get pulled around on a sled that was pulled behind a tractor. That lasted for quite a while and I remember
at nights I used to lay there and I couldn't sleep because me
back was itchy and I had no way of scratching it because it was
covered in plaster.

The next thing I remember was me first look at TV. We
were living in Coopers Plains in Bradman Street, and the bloke
a few doors down bought the first TV in the neighborhood and
used to charge people sixpence to go and have a look at it. The
first TV show I do remember seeing was about a frog and a
princess.

I remember the first TV I saw, was when we were living
on the Gold Coast, and we used to live at a house at the end of
a street with a tin roof, and I remember everyone got up there
on the roof and painted it red. Down the end of the street was
a little shopping center and people used to gather around the
shop window to watch TV, and I remember the whole lot of us
one night watching a horror movie. On the way home Mum
and all the grown up kids got home first and the little ones was
walking down the street looking at our house, when suddenly
all the lights went out at the same time. It was pretty scarey
and well, I wasn't about to stand around and wait. I was a
mile away down the road and someone else was stuck over the
gate, and someone was trying to climb the fence and they got
stuck, and someone else was trying to run in one spot (I think

that was you Wendy).

We moved to Redcliffe in the Scarborough area and I started going to the De La Sel College as a day pupil. They used
to have high red banks along the edge of the beach, with very
thick vegetation, and we used to have all these tunnels going
through it. We used to play chase's, and hide and go seek and
ambush other kids who were using it. At one stage I remember
Desley was in the tunnels and she found a 44 gallon drum, and
being smart like she was, she decided she was going to roll
this drum over the bank, and down below where there was a
couple making out; she rolled this thing down on top of them,
but fortunately it missed.

I used to like going to De La Sel College. We had a 50 meter
swimming pool and a picture theater and 13 football fields.
I played football for De La Sel, that's Rugby League, while I
was there as a junior and I also tried to get into the swimming
team but at the time I wasn't a very good swimmer. For some
reason I kept getting put in for breaststroke and I used to hate
breaststroke and I used to refuse to train.

I always thought Bribie Island was paradise, I absolutely
adored it. I used to run wild in the bush there and no one could
find me. I was usually always in the gun emplacements or two
miles up the beach doing something and there I was sent to De
La Sel for a week which used to happen to all the Catholic boys
on Bribie Island. Every year they'd pick so many to go to De
La Sel and I went and that week we have the swimming cham-
pionships against four other schools and I won six events, and

by doing that I was asked to go back and swim for De La Sel, which I did. After the first year with De La Sel I must have swam in about 30 swimming carnivals.

I had a great education. Every time, there was a class I didn't like I would get out of it by telling them I had to go to training. I think I must have been the best trained pupil there for swimming, because I tell ya, for Maths I'd go training, for English I'd go training, French I'd go training and it took about four months before the teachers woke up that there was no one at the swimming pool to train me and I was actually doing it by myself, and they just thought well this isn't on.

While I was at De La Sel, I joined the drum and bugle band which was quite good because I used to play the bugle and I used to be very good at it actually, and we used to do concerts and shows all around the place and we'd be away sometimes weekends. Also, at De La Sel we used to get day trips to Bribie Island to clean the scrub for the church and I used to always get picked because we only lived 4 houses from the church. So once a month I'd come home with about 12 or so of the college boarders and we'd be at the church clearing the bushes away from the grounds and after that we'd all go for a swim and spend a couple of hours at home.

I remember coming home for Christmas and Easter and all that, but I always felt like a stranger walking in through the house cause everyone had something to talk about and I didn't have much to say. I remember at the end of the first year, Monsignor Carley, he came round looking for Mum to ask me to go back to the school for another year. They actually wanted me for another 3 years but I met him at the front gate and told him that Mum had to go to Brisbane urgent and that she'd probably be there for a while, probably a week, and they had made their mind up that I wasn't going back to school because they needed me at home to earn money to help support the family.

While I was on Bribie Island I was working for a surveyor. We surveyed from Bongaree to Woorim, the south side of Bribie Island through all the bush, where there was all virgin swamp land and I used to love doing that. It was really thick mosquita bush and I remember when he finished he asked me if I wanted to go to New Guinie to help survey there, but Mum told him I was too young to go, so I never had a chance to shoot off.

My next job, I was working for OTC, (Overseas Tela Communications) halfway between Bribie Island and Caboolture. They put an OTC relay station up for long distance transmission and one of the towers was 150 feet, and I kept getting into trouble for climbing it. I wasn't allowed to climb because apparently I wasn't good enough and my job there was just to paint the towers, but they would only let me go up 60 feet. They wouldn't let me go up any higher and I did that for six months.

I got a job with another surveyor after that, redoing the same area that we had done before. I didn't like that surveyor though as good as the first one. He was a young guy and he seemed to know everything and he kept saying that the first

Surveyor made a mistake. Personally, I don't think he did but this young bloke was out to make a name for himself.

On Bribie Island, I joined the Bribie Island Surf Club as a cadet, and I remember me first patrol and we had two rescues and that's where I met Arthur (Teresa's husband) for the first time and I always thought Arthur was a superman. I used to watch him train and paddle and things like that, and I used to say I wanted to be just like Arthur and to me he was my hero and I've got a lot of time for Arthur and I reckon he's a terrific bloke.

He helped me in my younger days in the surf club. I used to sneak off and watch him train like I said and try and copy the way he paddled and the way he done things and I remember the first Iron Man's event I went in at Maroochydore, I won the swim and I won the board section but I was still doing the ski paddle when everyone else had finished. Before the ski leg had started I was probably 60 meters in front, but by the time I got off the ski I was probably 200 meters behind and 200 people had passed me. My first effort as an Iron Man didn't work out very well.

In the same carnival, I came third in a board paddling race. In those days there wasn't special long boards made for this event like there is now. They were just a normal surfboard that everyone rode, and I had me first surfboard that I bought that was by Dunlop (the tyre company). I got it through a catalogue order from Walton's store, and I remember coming in third in me first board paddling race, but I got disqualified because I lost me patrol cap.

I had a good time at Bribie Surf Club. I had plenty of bar-beques and there was dances and there was always something happening. The surf wasn't very good, it was the type of surf that you could sit on the beach and wait for a wave and then run out and catch it. I remember, we had an old Bulsar board, I think Arthur gave it to Teresa and it got handed around. It used to take two of us to take it to the beach and three of us to take it out of the water it used to be that heavy from being water logged.

From there we went to the Gold Coast, where I joined the Northcliffe Surf Club, and there I used to train quite a lot and I used to run some 15km a day and I used to paddle me board 5 or 6km a day and I remember I used to surf at sunrise and used to not come in until sunset. I sat there all day by meself and some days we had big surf and I remember one time we were catching waves from way out past the shark buoys and used to ride them into the shore break and the shore break used to be some 15 feet tall. That was quite an experience.

While we were at Northcliffe surf club we had a few res-cues and I remember one day I was talking to me girlfriend who lived at Brisbane one time, her name was Rita, and we was talking on the phone and a bloke come up and told me that his mate was drowning. Anyway, I grabbed me paddling board and went down the beach and started paddling out through some waves, and the waves were about 8 foot and when I got out there this guy was about 500 meters out and he was swimming the wrong way and I stopped him and asked him what he was doing and he said he was trying to get to shore.

He was quite well drunk and anyway, I put him on me paddling board which used to hold two people quite easy and when he hopped onto the board it went three inches under the water. Anyways, we got through the outside break first and a big wave came and we wiped out there, anyway I put him back on me board and when we got to shore and when he stood up he was about 6ft.5". No wonder me board sunk!

The next day these two Americans showed up and they were looking for the guy who pulled his mate out of the water. Anyway they pointed me out to them and I walked up and they told me they were aircraft pilots from the American Air Force and they were over here to do an air show, and they asked me if I wanted to go for a ride in their jet and I told them I wasn't allowed because I had to work on the beach.

Anyway, they wanted to know what they could get for us and at the time it was illegal for Playboys to be sold in Queensland, so one of the guys suggested they get us a Play-boy magazine, and so every month for about 2 years we had Playboy magazines sent to our club from America. It was about four or five months after that I received a letter from the American Government congratulating me on what I had done.

It was about mid winter of 1966 that we had a mass rescue on a day me and me friends from the club we were all out surf-ing and the waves were some 10 to 15 feet high, and it was a beautiful hot sunny day and the Gold Coast was absolutely packed with tourists. We had 42 rescues that day, and I did 15 of em meself, and another bloke did 10 and a few others did some and we had absolutely a busy day. It was early '68 when I was 19, that I decided to go to Sydney to try and get into the Olympic team which I didn't do very well at cause I didn't make the final cut. I moved to a place called Blacktown, where I met a girl called Vicki and we ended up getting married. I got a job there at the Blacktown swimming pool and I was there for 12 months and we moved to a place called Timmarimma, which is a beach just outside of Bondi and I remember the first week I was there, I walked down the beach with Vicki and the surf was about 20 feet high.

I wanted to go out for a body wave, because I didn't have me surfboard with me and she said there's no one out there and I said yes there is, there's a guy sittin right out the back and I'm gonna go out and join him. So I walked out to the cliffs and swam out from the cliff and got out there but the only thing that was out there was a marker bouy. It took me about 2 ½ hours to get back in and I actually thought a couple of times that I was going to drown.

I was down at Purina one Sunday afternoon, and the surf was nice and the surf club had a rescue on when three people out the back got pulled out in a rip, and while they were out there they had another rescue probably about a hundred meters off shore and there was no one to pull the people out so I swam out and pulled them both in. It turned out to be two young girls and the surf club went mad at me and told me I shouldn't have done it that I didn't know what I was doin.

I lived in New South Wales for some 7 years driving trucks and working in swimming pools and when I got sick of swimming pools I'd go back to truck. After that, me marriage broke up so I decided to drive west until I got to a beach called Scarborough Beach. That was as far as we could go, so I parked there and found a place to stay and I lived in a block of flats called Garfield Towers. I was there for about 4 months and there was a job advertised in the newspaper in a little town called Karoo for a pool manager, so I put in for it.

I went up there and I was up there for about 2 years and that's where I met me present wife Maxine. We been married 21 years, got a son, and I also got two daughters from Vicki.

Desley and Mum Christmas 2002

*Mum in 1970
at the age of 50*

Coral left, Dawn center, and Mum in 1955

Mum in 1999

Coral when she was 24, in 1963. with her husband Barney

Coral in 1957 at the age of 18

Coral and Barney 2003, enjoying their retirement together.

Dawn in 1959 at sweet 16

Dawn in December 2003

Dawn at the age of 10, in 1953

Teresa, 2003

Teresa in 1964

*Teresa 19, on her wedding day in 1966
with Coral 27 on the left, and Wendy 16.*

Wendy in 1958 at the age of 8

Wendy with Carol in December 2000, 6 months before Carol passed away

Desley in 1964, at the age of 13

Desley in 1998

*The famous gun emplacement where we all hung
out as kids. Desley in the foreground, 1964*

Carol in 1996
at the age of 42

Carol in 1960,
at the age of 6

From left to right. Coral 48 striped blouse, Mum 67 in back, Desley 36
front middle, Carol 33 behind Desley, Wendy 37, and Teresa 40 right.

Gary, the year before
he passed away in 1986

The younger boys of the family
From left to right.Gary 6, Tony 2, Shane 1, and Victor 4.

Victor in 1975, at the age of 19,
with his nephew Jeffrey

Victor and Coral in 1993

Bart with his wife Maxine

Bart in 1965, at the age of 16

Mum and Billy a year afer he had his brain haemorrhage

Shane 34 left, and Tony 35, in December 1992

From left to right, Gary 2, Desley 3, Wendy 4, Barton 5, Teresa 7, and Billy 8. Photo taken in 1954.

Teresa left, Wendy, and Coral right,
at Shannon Falls, BC, Christmas, 2003

The Bribie Island Pub, 1993

The house we all live in on Bribie Island.

A family photo taken in 1996, with Mum in the center.
Taken shortly after Billy passed away.

September 2001, The author and her three sons.
Jason left, Jeffrey back, and Wade right.

2004, Wendy with her husband Keith

CHAPTER SIXTEEN

Then there was me (Wendy)
(Born in 1950)

I'M THE MIDDLE ONE OF THE FAMILY, AFFECTIONATELY CALLED Princess by my father. I don't know where that came from, but my parents hardly ever raised a hand to me.

It's funny when you look back on life and find that things aren't always as they appeared, but it isn't until years later when reminiscing that you realize this. Take the day, when I was around seven, I recall us all sitting around eating potato skins that had been cooked in the open fire. I remember this day as if it was yesterday and at the time thought we were having a picnic, and it was a great adventure. It wasn't until Desley and I were recalling the past many years later that I found out that Mum didn't have anything for us to eat and this was in fact our dinner.

What shocked me more than anything was that Desley was younger than me, and at the time she knew the hardships Mum and Dad were going through and I didn't. Was it that I just didn't want to know, did I have my head in the sand, or was it just a great adventure.

We moved onto a dairy farm when I was around six, and I remember a creek down the back behind the milking shed, where Bob would throw the heads of the male calves after he chopped them off. He would let the mother suckle the baby long enough for her to develop a good milk flow, and then he would separate them from the cow and hit the male calf on the head with a large mallet. He would cut up the carcass for Mum to use and toss the head down into the creek for the catfish and crows to finish it off. The catfish grew plump and during the weekends we would go down to the creek to see if we could catch them.

Because it was a dairy farm, the female calves were spared the mallet and instead they were fed a mixture of grain and milk in order to build their bodies. Not long after birth the calves would be taken off their mothers teat and every morning before going to school and again on our return we would take buckets of milk up to the shed and feed them. They were so cute and in order to get them used to drinking from a bucket, we would let them suck on our fingers while lowering our hand into the milk. Eventually the calf would get the idea and when it was old enough it would be let out to pasture with all the grown ups. Ferdinand and Archibald were two huge bulls we had on the farm and were the sires of most of the calves born there during our stay.

I learnt to swim when Bob picked me up and threw me into the ocean, and it was either sink or swim. I soon got the hang of it, and although I didn't appreciate his training methods, it didn't take me long before I was willingly jumping in the deep end myself. When I was 8, I recall jumping off the end of the Scarborough Jetty, which was a swimming spot favored by the local residents. Scarborough itself was a popular tourist spot during the summer months, and visitors from everywhere would flock there with their families and partake in the activities the area had to offer.

The jetty, which was well known, was about 50 meters long and stood about four meters above the calm clear water. Bart and I were taking turns at jumping off the jetty in front of the visitors, but more for our own pleasure and afterwards we would quickly swim back to the steps to repeat our heroics. When it was my turn to dive however, I didn't think to check the water before diving and I landed on a Portuguese Man-O-War.

I remember seeing it just as I jumped and for a split second, being suspended above this huge slimy sea creature, with no way out. As soon as I hit the water it attacked me and I begun to struggle and scream with all my might. Looking back into the faces of those looking over the railing, I found it hard to believe that no one was coming to help me. In fact there were several young guys looking down at me laughing and I couldn't understand why, they must have thought I was pretending or something!

The pain was unbearable and the more I struggled, the more it enclosed me in it's long slimy tentacles. I soon found myself grasping at thin air just to breath and stay afloat, and while it seemed like forever, it was in reality only a few seconds before Bart jumped in and started pulling me to shore. Before I realized it, Mum was also by my side, pulling me in as fast as she could to get the thing off me. I was stung all over and was running out of breath when they put me in the back of a car and raced to the nearest ambulance bay.

On the way, I clawed at the open window for a breath of fresh air, and was relieved when they put the oxygen mask on me when we got there. I remember them rubbing me down with something to take the sting away, but as hard as they tried the pain remained, and it only started to subside after what seemed like hours.

The welts the creature left on my body were everywhere, and I recall sitting in a bath of cool water with Epson Salts to relieve the sting and swelling. In his effort to rescue me, Bart also received numerous stings under his arms, but as he was more concerned about me, he paid no heed to them. I don't know how long I took to recover but it seemed a long time, and I remember spending a lot of time in bed eating ice cream.

Thank God for the Catholic nuns and Father Marley. For many of our school years, we attended Catholic schools, and went to religious classes at those that were not. The Catholic communities, especially the churches, were a godsend to a large family, and Mum always knew she could rely on them when things were tough.

Almost always, at the beginning of each school year, she was able to completely outfit us with school uniforms, albeit second hand ones at that, and if we were really lucky, their generosity also included school books, pencils, rulers, pens and rubbers. For our part, we had to be good little Catholic girls and boys, which at times was a little difficult, especially with all those rotten State (Public) school kids walking past our school twice a day, and during their lunch breaks.

We were so disturbed by their irreverent behavior, repeated attacks, and smutty comments, that we composed our own song, which we proudly sung each time they passed.

> *State State sitting on a gate,*
> *Eating bellies out of snakes.*
> *State State sitting on a log,*
> *Eating bellies out of frogs.*

And even though they had a choice of which side of the street they could walk, just to annoy us, they deliberately came on our side. So we would sing our song out loud each time they passed, and soon claimed areas of land that was declared off bounds to them, even though it was outside of the school grounds. I often wondered what was in the minds of the town planners, to put a State school, and a Catholic school on the same block, let alone the same town. Don't they realize that the younger generations of these two establishments have a commitment of honor and loyalty that has been passed on from generation to generation for hundreds of years?.

Mum used to make the best school sandwiches and my favorite was toasted tomato. By the time I uncovered it from it's cellophane wrapping the tomato had soaked through the toast and the smell was something else. Another one of my favorites was Vegemite sandwiches, which I often ate along with the milk during morning recess. Of course as this was my only sandwich for the day, whenever I did this I missed out on lunch, so I was pretty hungry by the time dinner rolled around.

Even though I left everything to the last minute, and often didn't study, I never found school difficult, and in most of my classes, I sat in the back with the rest of the students the teacher believed didn't need constant supervision. I found this strange, as I hardly ever had to prepare for an exam, or cared to, and the kids in the back of the class were the ones who usually fooled around more than anyone else. They were simply lucky enough not to get caught; but sadly, one day, I wasn't so lucky.

The Catholic school we attended at Redcliffe had wooden floors that the nuns had meticulously polished by hand. To protect these floors from scuff marks, everyone who entered the rooms, had to either remove their shoes, or pull large football socks over them. Back then, we used ink nibs that you dipped into an ink well, which sat in a hole in the old wooden desks. As I sat in the back of the class, waiting for the rest of the students to finish an assignment, I became bored, and started playing with the ink well. The next thing, the whole thing fell over and onto the highly polished floor, and as the ink trickled down the desk, and the nun came running down to the back of the class, I literally saw my life flash before my eyes.

I could see the blood pumping through the veins in her neck, and she was so mad I thought she was going to rip my heart out with her bare hands. So I said three Hail Mary's, and prepared for the usual severe punishment that was common practice for such a crime. As she got closer, I could see the demon inside of her desperately wanting to escape, but she composed herself like a true professional, and calmly picked me up by my pigtails, pulled me to the classroom door, and told me to go home before she did something we would both regret.

It was only 10.30 in the morning, but who was I to argue, so I grabbed my bag and proceeded to walk home. It wasn't until I was nearly there that I realized why people were looking at me so strangely; I had left my football socks on, over my shoes.

Another day at the same school, I had finished another assignment, but instead of reading a book and keeping quiet, as instructed by the Nun, I started tapping my pencil to the beat of a familiar song in my head. Once again, she came down to the back of the class, grabbed me by my pigtails, and told me to wait outside. While I was waiting for the others to finish, I took my wooden ruler out of my bag, and proceeded to tap on the metal framework holding up the new covered walkways. Unbeknown to me, this new section of framework supported the walls throughout the new classrooms, which meant that tapping on one of them, caused an echo to vibrate through all three rooms of the new extension.

As I sat there honing my skills as a percussionist, out walked the three nuns simultaneously, and I swear, if looks could kill, all three would have gotten life. I was stripped of my instrument and sent home again, but I could never understand how this could be considered a form of punishment.

I had a habit of leaving things to the last minute, and one Christmas when I was thirteen, I did it once again. Before going on an eight-week Christmas break from school, our teacher had given us an assignment on horticulture and farm machinery. Cramming being my usual style, I still hadn't done anything by the Sunday night before school was to commence, so I waited until 9 o'clock that night, snuck out the window and ran to the house of the smartest girl in school Cathy Warner; who just happened to be a friend.

I tapped on her bedroom window, and when I explained my predicament, she soon had an assortment of books and magazines spread out on the floor for me to go through. I spent the next two hours in her room, sorting through and taking notes from the selection, and when I was finished I snuck back home. The next morning in school our teacher asked for our assignment, and was so impressed by mine, he gave me an A+ and asked me to read it to the class, and that year, I was awarded a prize for the best assignment.

Attending school in Australia was sometimes a hazardous undertaking, when during spring, the dreaded Magpie would bombard us as we walked to and from school. Well known for protecting its young to the extent of drawing blood, it would attack anyone who strayed within the boundaries of its nesting area. This incorporated a half-mile radius for each nest, and everyone knew the drill, which was to completely avoid the area all together if possible. This was at times unavoidable however, as most of the schools we attended had huge gum trees in which the Magpies nested.

For three to four weeks a year, when the fledglings were mastering their flying skills, the parents would dive-bomb anyone who walked within their boundaries. Like snipers waiting patiently until you got within firing range, they would dive bomb unannounced, and the only way to protect yourself was to wear a hat or put up a brollie. The old standby was a stick held high above your head, which we would wave frantically trying to stop the magpie from reaching its target. Sometimes however, in an effort to protect ourselves, the stick would connect with the bird and it would drop to the ground, and even though you were only trying to defend yourself, you felt like a real bastard, because there was now an orphan magpie chick up too high to retrieve and care for.

When I was around 10, we moved to Bribie Island, which is a small island community with a population of around 3,000 people at the time. I lived on Bribie until I was 16, and as there wasn't much for teenagers to do, every now and then Mum would take us to the local Saturday night dance; for lack of something better to do; most of the local kids went with their parents. We would all line up along the wall and pray that someone half descent would ask us to dance even if it was our own brother, it was better than one of the old fogies.

The Progressive Barn Dance was one dance I dreaded, because no matter who you started out with, you would always end up with someone else and of this you had no choice. It would inevitably be someone without teeth, and who after a few drinks, saw themselves as Fred Astaire and you as Ginger Rogers. Of course, whenever this happened, your friends would be on the sideline killing themselves with laughter about your predicament.

Mum was always trying to get all the girls in the family up to sing at these dances and from time to time, she would drag us up to entertain those attending. "Sisters, sisters, we were never more devoted sisters"; we would sing this, and back to our hiding places we would go,

Shortly after we moved to Bribie, I had my first cigarette. Fashioned from the ends of used cigarettes that Dad had tossed out the living room window, Gary, Bart, Desley and I would smuggle them over to the gun emplacements, where we would gently unroll them, and mold our own cigarettes using small pieces of newspaper. We would sit there for ages, pretending to enjoy them, like four seasoned smokers, familiar with the antics one acquires from years of the nasty habit. Even though they tasted terrible, none of us confessed or acknowledged at the time just how bad they really were; we thought we were so cool.

For some reason, Mum considered me a sensible person for a thirteen year old. One day she gave me her last $10 and told me to "go to the local shop and buy whatever I thought would get us through the next few days", until her next cheque came through. I was feeling quite grown up and proud as I ran into the shop to buy what I reckoned would get us through the next few days, and even though I had made what I considered was a great selection, when I gave Mum the shopping bag, she was as mad as hell. In it she found something for the windows, something for the floors, something for the washing and even toilet paper, and as Mum believed in good old fashion elbow grease, I'm sure she thought these items were a waste of money.

It seems that I thought it was more important to have a clean house, than to have food in our bellies. Needless to say, I was sent back down to the shop with a note to beg for credit until her next cheque came through. I don't know what all the fuss was about, after all we not only had food in our bellies, but also a clean house.

Once when things were really bad and we had been living on soup for quite some time, I went to the kitchen to find something to eat. I guess, I was around ten at the time and I was so hungry I could have eaten a horse. I was home by myself as Mum had gone out for a few hours. After looking in the fridge and through all the kitchen cupboards all I could find way at the back of one of them was one tin of peaches and one tin of cream. I thought she must have forgotten they were there, and won't notice if I just put a tiny hole in the can, and suck some of the juice out. I did this to the cream as well, and enjoyed the nectar of both cans for a few days. There was no guilt, after all, I was only sipping on the juice and a little of the cream and what harm could that do?

A few days later, Mum prepared something for dinner and as a special treat, she went to the back of the cupboard and got the two cans out. I was relieved to see that she hadn't noticed the two tiny holes and proceeded to open them. Everyone was sitting around the table waiting, and all of a sudden, she started to cry. When she opened the cans, both of them had green mold in them and she couldn't use them. I think she knew what had happened, but didn't ask who did it. To this day I haven't told her that it was me.

When I was in my early teens, I thought The Beatles were to die for, and although I didn't have any of their records, every opportunity I had I would collect pictures of them from magazines and paste them on my bedroom wall. They weren't very popular with Mum and Dad, but during their Australian visit, I was allowed to watch them on TV. As I sat on the floor watching them, straining to hear the broadcast of their visit, but all I could hear was criticism and laughter coming from behind me. The harder I tried to hear, the more of a joke it was for the others.

Their songs to me were the best and I got so mad I started to cry, but as I got up to go to my room, Bob grabbed me and pulled me to his lap. He apologized and his words were comforting, but I soon found that he had an ulterior motive for his kindness. His gesture soon grew to support his own needs and as I sat on his knee I could feel him grow. Shivers ran up my spine and the more I struggled, the harder he became and as I broke free I could hear his laughter, with those around us none the wiser about his actions.

Bob seemed to get great joy out of tickling me to the point of tears. Not that it was funny, but he put so much force into it, that it was painful. More than once he threw me on the bed, and in the process he became aroused. I would beg him to stop, and I would make so much noise that he had no choice but to let me go.

I wet the bed until I was fourteen, but the thing is, I knew many times that I was doing it. You see there were gremlins under my bed and as soon as I put my feet on the floor they would pulled me under, never to see my family again. Some nights I would wake up wanting so bad to go to the toilet, I didn't know what to do. Each time I would compare the wrath of the gremlins with Mum's temper and the gremlins always won. So if I couldn't hold it until morning, I would sneak to the bottom corner of the bed and pee on the outer covers.

Mum would congratulate me the next morning on having a dry bed, and I would go off to school feeling a little guilty, but still kind of relieved that I had gotten away with it again.

Of course it didn't take her long to seek out the source of the smell emanating from the room I shared with Desley. On the days that I did get caught, I would have to wash my sheets in the boiler and hang them out to dry before I went to school. Whenever I wet the bed, I always felt a sense of safety and comfort as if I was in a cocoon and if I had a choice, I would have laid there for the rest of my life, that is until I had to move and the lack of warmth got to me.

I remember when I was real young, Mum had gone into hospital to have one of the kids and left some of us with Dad's sister, Aunty Peggy. She knew I was a bed wetter and made me sleep in a cot with plastic lining and even though I stayed awake most of the night, way past the time when everyone else was asleep, I still wet the bed. She didn't like me and used to be nasty whenever Mum wasn't around, and when she found out that I had wet the bed, she called me a baby and did everything she could to embarrass me in front of everyone. If I could name one person I would consider the wicked step Aunt, she was it.

I left school and got my first job when I turned 14 on May 17, 1964. Back then, this was the legal age to leave school however, before leaving the school Head Master, Mr. Wiggins tried to convince, Mum that I had a brain. He said if I stayed, the school system would pay for my education all the way through high school. I wonder if the offer still stands?

We all had commitments back then to help out in the house, so as soon as I could, I was outa there and started looking for work. I wanted to do my part and was determined to find employment no matter what. My first job was helping out in the kitchen at the local pub on Bribie Island. Teresa worked there and put a good word in for me and it wasn't long after I left school that I started working there. We worked well together and every morning at 6 o'clock we would have to chop the wood and carry it to the kitchen at the back of the pub for the huge wood burning stove.

Teresa was responsible for the cooking when I first started working at the pub, but not long after I started there she got married and left and they hired someone else. After collecting the wood, I would have to start the fire, get the stove heated for the new cook and set the dining room tables. I always made sure there was plenty of wood, especially on Sundays, when they opened the garden at the back of the pub for Sunday drinkers. Otherwise if we ran out, the cook would make me walk past all of those boozers and cart it back, with them glaring and perving at me all the way.

He would expect me to have everything ready for him, as he stumbled through the door still smelling of liquor ten minutes before the dining room opened. Bacon, eggs, sausages, Bubble and Squeak, and toast laid out so all he had to do was throw them on the plates. I guess that's why they called him the cook. He had filthy habits, and if he was having a bad day, I would try to steer people away from certain foods that he had fouled in some way or another during the day. I caught him one-day put his finger against one nostril and blow his nose in the pea soup. I was so sickened by it, I did a technicolor yawn before I could go on. Every time someone asked for the soup of the day, I told them we had just run out. This was of course hard to explain to the first few customers, so I just told them the cook added the wrong ingredients and had to throw it out. At least I wasn't lying, after all, he did add the wrong ingredient, I just didn't tell them what it was.

One morning he just didn't show up, and as I had everything ready, I opened the dining room and started serving the guests. Fortunately, there were only a few hotel guests so we weren't busy, but I had to do everything, including waiting on the tables, and cooking each meal and pouring the coffee and tea. Cookie never came back and I looked after everything myself for a few months until it got too busy for one person and. I put a word in for my sister Desley; not long after that, she started working there as well.

Desley and I pretty well managed the kitchen and dining room ourselves, and whenever we weren't busy, we would hang out the dining room window and watch the people walk by. In the mornings we would talk to our friends as they waited for the school bus under the fig tree across the street from the pub. It wasn't that long ago that Desley caught the same school bus with them, but like me, she also left school as soon as she was old enough to go to work. The view from the window was always better on the week-end when the lifesavers would often walk past on their way to the only shop. It was while I was working at the Bribie pub, looking out of this very window, that I started talking to my first husband Carl, and not long after that we started dating.

My boss and his wife lived at the hotel in an upstairs room, and every morning after the hotel guests were served, I would have to take breakfast to their room; it was the same boring thing every morning. Two boiled eggs, white toast and tea. After preparing their breakfast one day, I went to their room and knocked, but I couldn't hear anything, so I knocked again. I thought I heard someone yell "Come in", but I guess not, because there they were, in all their glory, doing it doggy style in the middle of the room. Or did they say "I'm coming?"

I was a virgin, I'd never seen such a thing, and I didn't know which way to look. That was the first time I actually saw a man's penis, in full flight. Not that it had anything to do with it, but not long after that, they sold the pub and retired. I guess they wanted to get out into the country where they could really let loose.

The new owners were a young couple with big dreams, and they soon started remodeling the hotel. They also offered me a job behind the bar, which called for a pay rise of $2 a week plus tips. Of course I snapped it up, after all, how could I resist such an offer. At the time I was only 15, and although the owners knew that having someone so young behind a bar was against the law, that didn't deter them; after all, they knew the local police captain.

It didn't take long though before it was out about the new barmaid and the pub clientele soon grew, but my new position didn't go down too well with the wives and girlfriends of the men who frequented the place. Back then, ladies had their own area to drink in, and it was frowned on, and certainly not lady like, if you were caught in the open bar area. If you did, there was hell to pay, and you were soon sent packing back to your own area. As I worked in the bar and was just their lowly servant, I wasn't walking on hallowed ground, or breaking any sacred rule.

One Friday night, a few months after I started working behind the bar, there was a racket out the front, with wives yelling out for their husbands to get home. One of them even brought the mattress from their bed, and told her husband if he didn't come out, he could move into the pub, after all, he seemed to spend more time there than home lately. Of course, there was safety in numbers for both husbands and wives and no one was budging. The next thing, in walks a half dozen brave souls who proceeded to shackle themselves to the bar. It took a couple of hours to bring peace to order, and the pub closed early to have an emergency meeting. That night there was a compromise. I could continue working behind the bar and to the shock of some of the patrons, their hallowed domain was now open to everyone, including women.

I got $29 a week for that job, and gladly handed over all, bar three dollars, to help Mum out in the house. Back in those days, there wasn't any Government assistance or child endowment and Mum relied a lot on our pay cheque coming in to help out with the bills and food. I saved every penny of that three dollars, and the first thing I bought was a surfboard that I got through a mail order catalogue when I was 15. Before I got my own board I shared an old surfboard with my brothers and sisters. It was heaps of fun, but for some reason the boys always seemed to have it when the waves were good and the girls were left with it when there wasn't any surf.

My first car was a tiny Austin that my brother Bart and I went halves in. It cost us $20 each and even though I was too young to drive, I would jump in it, and zip up to the local shop for Mum, via the back roads. On one of my trips, I saw the local constable heading my way, so as we passed each other on opposite sides of the dirt road, I ducked down behind the steering wheel. I guess I wasn't thinking that a headless driver would be more noticeable than a full bodied one, and the next thing I'm being pulled over and given a tongue lashing. Mind you, this was the same constable who let a minor work behind the bar, so I thought it was hypocritical of him to start laying down the law now.

One day, Mum and Dad had friends over for a barbeque, and as I pulled into the yard I put my foot on the accelerator instead of the break. The next thing, I'm perched on top of the barbeque like a giant Oscar with everyone killing themselves with laugher. It was very embarrassing and took everyone to lift the car, with me still in it off the barbie.

It was during my fifteenth birthday party while playing spin the bottle on the beach that I had my first real toungy, which I thought was disgusting. I couldn't understand how such a move could turn anyone on, but mind you, the boy I had to kiss wasn't exactly Casanova, or my first choice at the party.

Not long after my sixteenth birthday, we packed up and moved from Bribie Island to a town 120 kilometers south called the Gold Coast. We were always behind in the rent payments, and as usual, to ensure we had a clean getaway, the move was planned for late in the evening. We rallied as many friends with cars as we could, and Bob borrowed a truck for the larger items. As we carried the boxes, and pieces of furniture to the cars and truck, the lookout saw the lights of a car coming up the dirt road and yelled out to warn Mum. It was around 10 o'clock and a beautiful clear night, when the next thing she turns the lights out, and tells everyone to freeze. Well there we were, all frozen in different stages of putting things into the cars, when along comes the property owner, Mr. Walner. It was so embarrassing; I thought I was going to die.

All of us, including our boyfriends, lit up like Christmas trees under the full moon, and captured in a state of suspended animation. Mr. Walner drove past so slow I swear I could have spat though one window of his car and out through the other, but I have a feeling he'd heard we were leaving, and was just making sure it was really true.

My first job on the Gold Coast was that of a waitress at a resort called The Beachcomber on famous Cavil Avenue, where every day I donned a floral sarong and bikini top, and waited on the hotel guests. Sunday evenings was Hawaiian Hula night at the Beachcomber, where we earned an extra $2 in our weekly pay cheque for taking part in the Hawaiian floorshow. After serving dinner, we would dress up in grass skirts and bikini tops and like something out of a South Pacific movie, we would swing our hips to the delight of the hotel guests.

I used to take my surfboard to work and store it under the resort steps, and every day between breakfast and lunch, when I had a few hours to spare, I would go down to the beach surfing. I loved going to the beach, and rode a surfboard until late into my pregnancy with my first son Jason. When I fell pregnant, the Beachcomber manager transferred me from the dining area to housekeeping where I worked until I was eight months pregnant. Cleaning bathrooms, making beds and turning mattresses was a lot harder than serving tables, but I guess they were more concerned about appearance than my health.

Anyway, I still rode my surfboard and when I became too big to lay down, I kneeled instead, and when that was too much I just went to the beach and watched everyone else surf. I would dig a big hole in the sand to rest my belly in, and lie there for hours, sometimes falling asleep until Jason got sick of being in the same position too long, and would give me a little kick to remind me, "it's time to go Mum."

Sometimes, these trips would be rather humourous, when a young surfer, not realizing that he was only looking at half of me, would start flirting. That was until I stood up, at which time they would either get ribbed by their friends, or were too embarrassed to look. Of course, there was the odd occasion when some gorgeous guy would be sitting nearby, and I didn't want to stand up, but I would get a gentle reminder from Jason and off we'd go home.

After moving away from home, we always lived not far from my mother and siblings and we have remained a very close nit family ever since.

CHAPTER SEVENTEEN

My memories of my sister Desley
(Born in 1951)

T HE TOMBOY OF THE FAMILY, Desley was always getting into trouble, but she would do anything for you. She had a beauty about her I admired, that wasn't only physical, but also mental, and she had great strength and finality in her decision-making. We were only one year apart and became even closer when our own children were growing up.

When we were young Mum was forever cleaning the house, and she would go to great lengths to make sure everything was sanitized and sparkling. This included the drains in the house, which she doused weekly with a caustic solution. She would pour the caustic soda down the pipes and flush it out with hot water. This created a mountain of foam at each exit around the house, and on one of these cleaning binges, Desley and I were downstairs near one of the drain exits. I guess we were around three and four at the time and were ecstatic to see the free flowing ice cream coming from the drains; we soon had spoons in our hands scooping up the lather for a delicious treat.

I realized right away that this wasn't a good thing, but it took Desley several more mouthfuls before she experienced the burning. The inside of my mouth didn't suffer as much damage as Desley's and we both learnt a valuable lesson that day. Just like money doesn't grow on trees, ice cream doesn't flow freely from drains. Every second word from Desley's mouth when she was growing up was the F word (now affectionately called the in and out word), and I often wondered if this had anything to do with her caustic tongue.

She hated school, and often wagged it, and one day as we all headed off for the 4-mile trek both Desley and Gary complained all the way. Although we tried to persuade them otherwise, by the time we got to the school, they had convinced each other that they would be better off not going. All day, they hid in the bushes about a half-mile from school and were still hiding out when we passed by in the afternoon. They joined us as if nothing had happened, and when we got home, Mum was none the wiser about their day. We didn't dob on them, but the next day the teacher gave them both letters to give to Mum, which they promptly tore up, and that was the last of it.

One day, our youngest sister Carol made Desley miss

school, but this was one time she would rather have gone, than to endure what she did. She had dressed for school and with a few minutes to spare, decided she needed to go to the dunny at the back of the house. Rather than sitting on the cold seat and getting her bottom dirty, Desley had a habit of squatting on the seat with both feet planted on each side of the throne. While sitting in this rather precarious position, Carol pushed the dunny door open and it scared Desley. She fell in, with both of her feet going into the drum, right up to her thighs, and as the drum hadn't been emptied that week, it overflowed and Desley soon smelled as foul as the language coming from her mouth. Mum noticed the commotion and ran outside threatening to string Desley up if she made one step towards the house. She grabbed the hose and doused her until all signs of human feces was gone, but as she was wearing her only pair of shoes, much to Desley's delight, she got to stay home again.

We had the luxury of sharing the 8 feet x 10 bedroom after Teresa got married and moved out, and in it we drew an invisible line down the middle. We decorated within our boundaries the way we liked, and she plastered pictures of her favorite stars and singers on her side, and I put my favorite (the Beatles) on mine.

One day we got into a hair pulling match that sent us around in circles for quite some time, holding on for dear life to each others long mane, with both of us refusing to give in. Mum finally separated us, and we went our separate ways, vowing to never speak to each other again. One thing I've learnt over the years, is that Desley has a memory like an elephant. She never forgets anything, and quite some time after the battle, I came home from school and found that she had painted moustaches and beards on all of my Beatles photo's. I was so pissed off, I could have scratched her green eyes out. The funny thing was, the Beatles had changed their style of music and were just about to put their Sergeant Pepper Album out, so my pictures could stay.

We were only one year apart and when we were in our early teens we attended the Bribie Surf Club Saturday night dances together. The club was only a couple of kilometers away from our house, and we would head down while it was still light outside, with a warning from Mum and Dad that we had to be home by 10 or else. One night, we were necking with a couple of the lifesavers on the beach and as I looked up, there on the top of the sand dunes were the silhouettes of Mum and Dad. I almost shit myself and nudged Desley to get her attention. We hadn't been watching the time and both realized that it must have been past 10, and they had come down to the club to drag us home.

After they disappeared, we excused ourselves and hoping to get back before them we bolted up the beach towards home. Noticing when we arrived that their car wasn't in the driveway, with great relief we brushed the sand off our feet, jumped into bed, and waited for their return. Within a few minutes they were home, and we could tell their temper was at a boiling point by the way they slammed the doors of the car. As we laid there waiting for retribution, we could hear every step they made up the stairs and through the house, all the way to our bedroom. Although only one year younger than me, poor Desley couldn't get away with anything and she bore the brunt of the punishment. She was pulled out of bed, and both Mum and Dad gave her a hiding she would never forget.

Desley slept on the top section of a bunk we shared and as they threw her back into bed, still pretending to be asleep, I braced myself for a similar fate. Suddenly a hand stroked my forehead and Mum whispered to Dad that I was asleep, and they walked out of the room with Desley sobbing. Relieved, that I had avoided their outburst, I felt a sense of shame and remorse at Desley receiving a whipping ample enough for the two of us.

We lived a few streets from each other when we were married, so we often visited each other. She had a real knack of getting rid of unwanted visitors and one day, as she was standing at the kitchen sink doing the dishes, she notices a religious group doing their rounds. At the time the kids were keeping themselves busy in one of the bedrooms, and Desley says, "bloody Mormons, I'll get rid of them". The next thing, she's screaming out the side door as loud as she can. " You f***ing kids get your F***ing arses in here or I'll f***ing beat the shit out of you". She comes back into the house, and looks out the kitchen window again to see the Mormons running out the front yard as if they'd seen the devil himself. I guess they figured that she was beyond saving.

Desley and her husband Alan, had four beautiful children, Alan, Leanne, Adam and William. One day, when they were visiting their grandparents, William who was around 20 months old at the time climbed onto the bed and up onto the dresser. He leaned against the fly screen and the next thing he was on the cement 3 story's below. Leanne came running out of the bedroom and before the words were completely out of her mouth, her grandfather jumped over the three balconies down onto the grass in the front of the apartments. When he reached William his head had swelled to the size of a watermelon and it was obvious that there was serious damage.

An ambulance was called and he was taken to the Southport Hospital but they didn't have the equipment for such a serious head injury, and in an effort to save him, he was rushed by ambulance to the Brisbane Hospital, 80 kilometers away. They reached it in record time; a trip that usually took over an hour in those days, took 35 minutes due to a police escort and road blocks at all of the major intersections along the way.

William was in intensive care for 6 weeks and was prayed over several times, with each time Desley thinking it would be his last. I'll never forget the first time I saw Des when we arrived at the hospital after the accident. She looked dazed and confused; not ready to believe that this was happening. William eventually recovered but had to go on medication to stop epileptic fits.

Several years after William's accident the family took a trip to Bali for two weeks and each of the children were given

$10.00 spending money. This was to have lasted them the entire two weeks, and was quite a large sum of money for a 7 year old, but he immediately went shopping on the first day there to buy something special. On his return from Bali, he said to me "Aunty Wendy, if I give you this ring, will you wear it?" "Of course I will" I said, and as he handed it to me I commented on it's beauty. It had a silver band and blue stone and as I put it on my finger he said, "You have to wear that forever, and if you take it off you have to pay me $100:00". That was almost 24 years ago and I'm still wearing Williams ring today. I love all of my nieces and nephews, and William holds a special place in my heart.

Desley had a fantastic outlook on life and no matter how bad things were for us she always had a positive attitude about it. She isn't one to sit around and watch someone else do the work, and to this day no matter where she is, she will roll up her sleeves and chip in. I have a feeling though that she would prefer to do this than to sit around chin-wagging and having to make conversation. At least if she's kept busy she has an excuse

CHAPTER EIGHTEEN

Desley's memories of her childhood.

I WANT TO TELL YOU ABOUT MY BROTHER, who was classed as the outlaw of the family. His name was Gary and he was two years younger than I, and I was so proud of him, nothing scared him and he was my hero and I looked up to him.

I remember living on a farm that our father was looking after at Goomeri and I was only eight years old and Gary was six. We had two stud bulls named Ferdinand and Archibald who were huge, and I'm sure Gary only came up to their knee caps. Mum would send Gary off to the dairy across the paddock with the bucket for the milk and instead of following the dirt road around their enclosure, he would jump the fence. Next minute, we'd hear Gary yelling and there he would be swinging the bucket at the charging bully and guess who would win. Nothing scared my hero, and we always ended up with our milk.

In 1960 we moved to a little tropical island called Bribie, just off the coast about an hours drive from the city of Brisbane. Our house was very tiny for a family of eleven and it only had a few bedrooms. All girls in the one and all boys in the other but Mum used to cram as many beds as she could in the rooms and we slept head to toe. By the time I was twelve, at the age of wanting to explore (playing doctors and nurses,) I would ask Gary to be the doctor. We would end up kissing and cuddling and we were in our own little world. My hero, and me, nothing was going to ruin it and we were going to be together for a lifetime.

Then one day our whole world fell apart when Mum caught us coming out of the house and me fixing my blouse. I remember her asking me what we were doing and I told her we were looking for a spider that ran from under the mat. We knew she didn't believe me, so needless to say, we never played our game again. I think children learn from their growing years, and it is good to explore, to learn, and I know I have learnt a lot.

In 1986 we lost Gary in a tragic car accident and how our world fell apart. We loved him so much and we did not get time to tell him how much we cared. It's so unfair, it wasn't his time. He would do anything for anyone and he'd put everybody else before himself. He was my hero. Gary left behind two wonderful children, Corie and Becky, and the most beautiful wife Gay. If only he could see them now, he would be so proud. Corie has just got married and doing well, and Becky, has had two beautiful grandchildren.

There are so many things that happen to a family in a lifetime, not just mine but everybody, and not a day goes by when I think of something that happened in the past. All my family has been very close, and I pray for every one of them. I want so much to go back, to say I'm sorry if I ever hurt anyone. I know I can't but at least I have my memories, and no one can take that away from me.

One of my favorite places when I was young was a place called Coopers Plains. It was a great place to explore, especially when it was the weekend and it was a place when I wished time would stand still.

We had our own swimming hole in the bush, where we would go and catch yabbies and tad pole hunting, and bush walking to my favorite place, the local dump. Gary and I loved the dump, and the things we use to find. One day we came across this guy dumping a big bag so we waited behind a tree until he left, and went over to see what he had left behind. We were so excited but the bag was so heavy the two of us couldn't lift or drag it, so we went home and got the other kids to give a hand.

When we got back to the dump, Barton opened it up and it was like pigs to a trough, it was full of jellybeans. We sat around stuffing ourselves silly and that night we couldn't eat dinner, and to this day, 43 years later, I still can't stomach jellybeans.

When Carol was about 12 years old, I tried to explain to her about the birds and bees, but she told me she knew more about them than I did. At the time I didn't know she was being molested and I thought she was just kidding. So I sat her down and tried to explain by telling her about kissing, and she said it was dirty, and that you spat into each other's mouth. I asked her where she had heard that and she said at the movies, and I told her that it was a natural thing to do and that she will discover it as she got older. Then I tried to explain love balls, and how they affect the guy, and how you should not tease them, because it's a hard thing for them to control. She thought I meant tease the balls, not the guys.

When I tried to explain about sex I thought I could explain everything, but I got stuck and couldn't find the words. Carol just giggled and said, "I know what you are trying to say, I saw Mum and Dad piggy backing on the bed, and it's called root-ing". I was just trying to protect her as Mum never told any of us girls about the birds and bees and we learnt ourselves.

Remember the gun emplacements on Bribie Island and how we used to go into the many tunnels? I had better explain, a gun-in-placement is a huge concrete building built into the sand dunes on the beachfront. They were round and had many tunnels and rooms to house our soldiers, and they were built during World War 2. They had huge guns mounted on top, just in case of an invasion, but they were never used thank god, except by the local kids years later. We used it as a hideout, and to try and spy on any lovers who crawled in them.

At one end of the main tunnel someone had done a painting of a snow-white skeleton on the wall, and the room was as black as coal when you entered it. All you could see when you entered the room was this skeleton and we used to shit ourselves, it was so real. I remember our younger brother Tony was so shy, and one day we grabbed him and shoved him in the tunnel. It took him a long time to get over that. Gary and I used to hide our cigarettes in there and any grog his mate could get. We used to dig a hole and bury them and put a stone as a marker and at one time we had six cartons of ciggies and four bottles of rum hidden, and if anyone came near, we'd sit still and moan like a ghost. Sometimes it worked.

We moved around a lot and once lived at a place called Redcliffe. I liked it there and I had this special friend, but I felt sorry for her because her father used to beat her. I forget her name now, but she was really nice, and she told me one day that she was going to run away and asked me to go with her. She liked her grandmother who lived in Brisbane, about ½ hour away by car. I said I would go with her so we planned to do it on Saturday afternoon because Mum and Dad was going to a dance, and we would get to Brisbane before they got home. I told you Wendy and you tried to talk me out of it. I was determined to go so you dressed me up like a grown up and wrapped my doll in a shawl like a baby, and made some sandwiches and off we went.

By the time we got two blocks away we were hungry so we ate the sandwiches and started to hitch hike, but every time a car pulled up we'd run away. We had some coins, so decided to call a taxi, and when we got in he asked us where we were going and we said Brisbane. We got to one of the main streets in Brisbane (George Street) and he asked for the address. All my friend could remember was, "you go around the corner and up the hill". Well this went on for over an hour and he was getting so pissed, he took us to the police station.

I said I was eighteen but I know they didn't believe me, so needless to say we were driven home in a police car. By this time Mum was home and I thought I'd get murdered, but she just grabbed me and kissed me and asked me WHY? I told her about my friend and how I felt sorry for her and why, and the next thing she's living up in Brisbane with her grandmother. At least she got her wish.

I went back to Bribie last year to see if the gun-in placements were still standing, but the sands of time had taken over, and I stood there and pictured all of us sun baking and having fun on the top of it. Our old house is still there but it looks a lot different now, the whole island does.

If only we could go back, I do often in my mind.

CHAPTER NINETEEN

My memories of my brother Gary
(Born in 1952)

GARY WAS THE MALE OF THE family who was always getting into trouble, and although he was a year younger than Desley, he had the mind of a street smart kid twice his age; albeit a mischievous one at that. He was a real character, he would do anything for you and he was forever in the sin bin. Desley and Gary, were the water rats of the Clarke family. I mean this in an affectionate way, but they were the ones who would steal for you, lie for you, and probably if they had to, die for you.

One day, Desley didn't want to go to school again and would do anything to get out of it. She was in grade three at the time and she told Mum all kinds of stories to get out of going. At the time we lived in a big old house with a dunny out back, and Gary told her to go down the back and wait in the dunny for him. A few minutes later, he came down with a mixture of beetroot juice, milk, and left-overs, and proceeded to pour it all over the toilet seat. Then he goes running up to the house yelling out at the top of his lungs, "Mum, Desley was sick all over the toilet", and guess what, she got to stay home again.

Gary loved snakes, and one day he came home with a huge Carpet Snake. Mum refused to let him keep it, but after many hours of begging, he convinced her that he would be able to look after it and more importantly keep it out of her way. He had a great rapport with wild animals and would walk around the yard with the snake wrapped around his neck or watch TV with it curled up on his lap.

One night, Carol brought a boyfriend home and after everyone went to bed they turned the light out and started necking on the couch. Next thing, there's a scream coming from the living room (from Carol's boyfriend) and he's running out of the house, followed by a ball of dust. Apparently, the snake being as affectionate and used to humans as it was, was crawling up his leg onto his lap. Needless to say, that relationship didn't last long.

At the time we also had a cat that just had kittens but we couldn't find them. As they were only about 4 weeks old, we knew they couldn't have gone far, so we checked our yard and the neighbors, but they were nowhere to be seen. The neighbors kid came back to our place to help find the kittens and as we walked under the house and scanned the rafters, there it was, Gary's Carpet snake, stretched out along the beam, and looking as content as the three kittens, before he consumed them; his five-foot frame with three prominent lumps in his stomach that were obviously his last supper. The maternal instincts of the female members of the search party immediately kicked in, and if it weren't for Gary throwing his body between them and his snake, a caesarian section would surely have been performed that day.

Gary was Carol's shadow. Only one year apart, they spent a lot of time together when growing up, and one day when the dunny collector was making his weekly rounds, they decided to play a trick on him. He went to the back of the house with the empty tin, to replace the full one, but on his return, he didn't notice that Gary and Carol had set a trap. They had strung a piece of rope across the walkway, and as he walked past them with the full tin, they pulled it tight, tripping him and spilling shit everywhere. There was hell to pay when Mum found out, and even though we knew who did it, no one would tell so the whole lot of us had to clean it up. We figured that was the neatest trick, and was well worth the trouble everyone got into.

As long as it was self inflicted, Gary's pain tolerance was incredible, and I recall many a time when he would have a toothache so bad, but rather than go to the dentist, he would pull the darn thing out himself. He knew the importance of getting the whole tooth out, and his instruments of destruction often included a pair of pliers to get a good hold on the tooth and a screwdriver just in case he didn't get it all out the first time. He dreaded going to the doctor, and again would rather mend his own wounds than have someone else do it. If he cut his leg, out would come the needle and thread from Mums sewing kit, and he would do the best blanket stitch that he proudly boasted would guarantee an 'A' from his sewing class teacher at school.

He was a real character, always coming up with ways to find a quick buck. He and his wife Gay and their two kids Corrie and Rebecca, had moved into their new house, which they built brick by brick, and shortly after they decided to hold a house warming party. He was one to put everything into anything he did, and as part of the activities, he organized a toad hopping competition. The idea was to put a dozen toads in the middle of a large circle on the ground, and release them. Each toad had a number painted on its back, and everyone could place a bet on the toad they thought would get to the outside of the circle first. After painting the numbers on their backs, he put the toads in a bucket with a lid so they couldn't hop away. Imagine everyone's shock when the bucket was emptied and none of the toads moved. Gary had painted the numbers on with lead paint, and all of the toads died of lead poisoning. All bets were off of course!

If he could embarrass you in front of people he would, and one day as I was going through the '9 items or less' checkout counter in Woolworth, he started making a scene. He pretended he didn't know me and reported to the checkout operator that I had in fact 11 items not 9, and therefore was not entitled to go though the '9 items or less' checkout counter. As I tried to explain that he was my brother, the other customers standing in line also started counting my groceries, and as each one finished, you would think by the looks on their faces that I was standing there naked. As I did in fact have 11 items, the checkout operator had no choice but to ask me to move on. Gary of course did one of his vanishing acts, and was nowhere to be seen.

Because of his frequent jovial antics, I sometimes found myself trying to avoid him in shops. One day, as I was walking though the Pacific Fair Shopping Center, I noticed him coming from the opposite direction. I wasn't in the mood for his clowning around and as he got closer, I turned my back to him so he wouldn't recognize me. As he walked past, I saw his reflection in the shop window and I felt a sense of shame at what I had done, so I quickly turned around and pretended that I had only just seen him. We went for coffee and had the best conversation in a long time. How could I do such a thing? Ignore my brother for fear of being aggravated or embarrassed by him.

A few days after our get together, Gary was killed in a car accident and I recall vividly the day it happened and how I found out about it. My first husband, Carl was downstairs talking to a neighbor, just chin-wagging about their day. I was listening in, and the neighbor had gone into great detail about a horrific accident he had just witnessed. How they tried, but couldn't get the guy out of the burning car. I went upstairs to take myself away from the graphic explanation, and as the news was just about to start, I turned the TV on. The phone rang and it was Gary's wife Gay, crying uncontrollably and saying something about Gary. I couldn't make out what she was saying, until I looked up and saw what was left of his car in the news headlines.

Three weeks after Gary passed away, I got a call from Gay. She was having trouble going to the wardrobe in which she hung her's and Gary's clothes, and asked if I could come over to help her clean out his belongings. I agreed, and the following Saturday I went to their house, but as I walked in Gay passed me in the doorway declaring that I should get rid of "EVERYTHING"; all of his clothing and personal items had to be gone on her return, and the only thing she wanted to see were the family photo's on the walls.

As I went through his clothes I pressed each and every article against my face and inhaled with all my might the odor of his body that still mingled in them. At one point during the day it got too much for me, and although I thought it was all in my mind, I yelled out and cursed God for doing this to us. I didn't realize I had been so vocal until one of Gay's neighbors came over to see if I was ok.

After putting everything of Gary's in several plastic bags, a thought came across my mind, " Oh my God, how could I give all of his belongings to perfect strangers", so I emptied everything onto their bed, and searched for something of his that I could keep. I selected three items from the assortment of articles; a packet of cigarettes, an old white Sloppy Joe with the words "Bad Boy" on the front, and a boy scout's leather tie band. Each of the items I chose had a special meaning.

On my way home from Gay's that day, I went out of my way to find a Lifeline store that I knew our family wouldn't frequent, and as I took the bags of Gary's clothing out of the boot of the car, a lump formed in my throat, that I thought I wouldn't survive. That was the hardest thing I have ever had to do, and I was overcome with grief. How could something like a piece of clothing be so overwhelmingly important?

Several weeks passed before I saw Gay again and she thanked me for helping her with Gary's clothes, but she also felt a great deal of remorse for having thrown everything away.

She expressed her regret of not having something of his and as much as I wanted to keep them, I told her about the items I had kept. I could see the pain she was still going through, and as soon as I gave them to her she started to cry. Although I had chosen the three items based on my own needs, each of them had a special meaning to her. The cigarettes because Gary always wore them on his sleeve just like James Dean, the Sloppy Joe because it was something he always wore around the house for comfort, and the boy scouts tie because it brought back memories of the times he spent at scouts with his son Corrie.

Gary was 34 years old when he died, and I miss him very much and think of him often.

CHAPTER TWENTY

(Gary)

When Gary's wife Gay, found out I was doing this journal, she asked if she could do Gary's chapter, and the following was written by her.

AS GARY IS NOT HERE TO TELL HIS STORY, I hate the thought of him missing out, so I would like to tell it for him. As his partner of 12 years, I knew and loved him for over a third of his short life. I won't go into his childhood, as I wasn't there, and his brothers and sisters have already told much of their memories from that time.

I was 14 when I met Gary, he was 20. I was working in a record shop in Broadbeach on the Gold Coast, on Saturday's and school holidays, I had put my age up to 15 in order to get the job, thankfully I looked a bit older than my age. Gary was a lifesaver at the local club, my shop was very close to his club and also where he lived, which was in a flat underneath his sister Wendy and her family. He had spent a small fortune in unwanted records, (in order to get my attention), before I noticed him. He had no front teeth (they had been knocked out in some fight), very short spiky hair on the top of his head, and very long at the sides and back.

As a typical surfy of the day in 1974 he only ever wore board shorts, these were never to be washed in a machine, only in the surf while he was surfing, and a pair was never discarded while they still had the ability to stay on, regardless of how many holes and rips were in them. He was a sight to behold, but he had a cheeky grin and a smile that could light up a room, despite the missing teeth.

We became good friends, I had no romantic notions about him at this stage, the age difference was too great, and I was actually going out, (as we called it) with one of his friends, and on more than one occasion it was Gary that patched up a tiff between the two of us. It was a few months before I realised he was interested in me as more than a friend, by this time I had got to know him fairly well. I started going out with Gary, but at 14 I had no interest in sex, and he quickly dropped me for a more willing partner. I was devastated, for about a week, as you are at 14.

It was six months before our paths crossed again, by this time I was the ripe old age of 15, and we started going out again. It didn't take long to realise we were both hopelessly in love. He used to come to my home every night and bring a bag of marrella jubes for me, which he usually proceeded to eat himself. My parents, were worried about his age, so I told them he was 19. A month later I told them he was really 20. And then one day he accidentally told them about what he'd done on his 21st birthday. But they had become very fond of him and accepted him as one of the family.

We desperately wanted to live together, I used to sneak out my bedroom window and walk to his flat at night, and return early in the morning, always taking my dog Ben with me (which Gary had given me as a puppy), If I got caught coming home in the morning, I would say I was taking the dog for a walk on the beach. Gary came up with the great idea of getting pregnant, that way my parents would let us get married. It sounded like a good plan, so thats what we did. I fell pregnant in October 1974 in my tenth year of high school. Christmas, of the same year my parents decided to take our family to Tasmania for 2 months over the holiday's. The separation was too much for us both, and Gary sold most of his possessions, including his car, to buy a plane ticket and come and join us at the family farm we were staying at.

This raised quite a few eyebrows in the quiet Tasmanian back town. He got a job bailing hay with some of my cousins and it wasn't long before he fitted into farm life and had won the hearts of everyone with his quick witted and quirky ways. One of my Aunties, who was very straight in her ways, took an instant liking to Gary and became great friends. She reminded me recently of something Gary said to her at this time. For some reason that she can't remember, Gary was extremely angry at her, but instead of swearing at her, he told her that he hoped her eye balls would turn into bum holes and shit all over her face. At which they both laughed, and forgot the dispute.

After returning from Tassy, I was beginning to show and we decided it was time to tell the "oldies". To our surprise they had already guessed, and gave us their blessing. We had to wait until I turned 16 in March before we could legally get married. Our wedding was a backyard bar-b-que affair, very informal, but the best thing about it (apart from getting married) was that all of Gary's family was going to come. This would be the first time since anyone could remember, that they would all be together at one time. The only other time since then was at Gary's funeral. The only family member missing from these two occasions was his father, who was invited but never acknowledged the invitation on both occasions.

At our wedding, it broke Gary's heart that his father was absent, so a couple of months later we decided to drive to Gympie to see his dad. I was eight months by this time, and remember the drive well, it took nearly 24 hours instead of the usual 4, because of the car breaking down all the way. Gary hadn't seen his dad since he had returned home with Barton to their mother, after leaving Billy with their dad. He was so excited that he could see him again.

Unfortunately, this excitement wasn't returned, and after

many attempts by Gary to start a relationship with his dad again, he had to finally admit that his father just didn't care. He looked upon Gary as part of a pile of kids he once had in his younger years, a pile of kids that were just too much trouble to keep up with. If only the silly man realised how much he missed out on. The only person to keep in contact with him was Coral, the eldest. I'm sure whatever he needed in his life as far as the advantages of a doting child goes, he got from Coral, so he didn't need the rest.

Our son Corrie was born in July, followed by Rebecca two years later. They were a constant source of joy for Gary, he was a great father, he loved the noise and chaos of a house full of children, reminding him of his own childhood.

Looking after a household and two small children at 18 might sound daunting to some people, but it was a breeze for me, because I had the support of the Clarke family. Most mornings I could be found at one of Gary's sister's tables drinking coffee and gossiping, usually accompanied by two or three other sisters and his mother, Thelma. They were a very close family and included me in everything. Most conversations for the day would start with, "Guess What?" From there we would talk for hours with all our kids playing outside or on our knees. Many stories were told and retold about past events when they were children.

Gary, although a very hard worker, only found the necessity to work as many hours as it took to pay the rent and buy food. The rest of the week he would take off to surf and spend time with the kids and I. I guess he was a typical bricklayer, unreliable! We never felt the need for material possessions, we were happy with our priorities. This changed unfortunately, as we got older and more responsible.

Life with Gary was terrific, I never regretted for a moment the normal teenage life I had abandoned. People say once someone close to you has died, you only remember the good in them and forget everything bad, but there was a bad patch that I remember vividly.

Gary had a condition which used to give him fits or seizures. Although he had had many cat scans, the doctors could never say he was epelepitic, just that he had abnormal brain waves. I remember one Saturday, he went to his sister Coral for the weekend at Redland Bay, to build her a fireplace in her new home. He was always doing freeby's for family and friends. On the Saturday night he took a seizure, a bad one lasting for over an hour. Coral and her husband didn't know what to do, so they rang an ambulance.

The ambulance drivers refused to take the still fitting Gary with them unless Coral signed a form. She was in distress at watching Gary, and signed the form so he could get to hospital. The form she signed put him in a mental hospital in Brisbane for 30 days, not to be released while he was being assessed.

I arrived at the hospital the next morning and found Gary in a padded cell with a straight jacket on, still doped out by the massive amount of Valium they had given him. My pleas were unheard by hospital staff to release him, they said once the form was signed their hands were tied. He had to stay.

My father consulted a solicitor, he also said he could do nothing. I know Gary wasn't ill or mentally unstable when he went in, but he became that way by the time he left. The doctor's convinced him he had unsolved problems, that maybe caused the fits. The other patients told him that once you came to a place like this you always returned, and that this was just the start for him. He came out in a deep depression, that he couldn't shake.

Fed up one day, I told him I didn't like living with a psycho any more than he liked being one. I gave him the option to shape up or ship out. He said if he could get away, far away from the hospital he was dreading going back to, then he should feel alright again. So we sold our first home, which we'd only just finished building; packed the car and drove to Perth to live. It was the most far away place we could think of and as soon as we left the cloud lifted from above him and I had my old Gary back again. It was the best thing we could of done.

Barton was the only person we knew in Perth, and he was thrilled we were coming over. He also had a love of surfboard riding, and the two of them were inseparable during the three years we lived there, before coming home again. The night before we left to come home I found Bart and Gary crying in each others arms, neither realised it would be the last time they saw each other, Gary was killed a year after we returned home.

During his last year, Gary was driving over Burleigh Hill one day when he spotted a koala on the side of the road, in danger of being run over by the heavy volume of traffic on the road. He pulled over, picked the koala up and put it on his back seat. He was always rescuing animals of some sort, usually snakes which Corrie also inherited his love for. He drove off intending to take it to the sanctuary, it looked like it had the eye condition that sends them blind.

Not long after driving off, the koala leaped off the back seat and attached itself to Gary's head, clawing his face and chest to pieces. He managed to pull over, but couldn't get the koala off his head. Eventually he rolled on the ground and freed himself, then grabbed a blanket from the car and wrapped the koala up (very tightly) and threw it in the car. He decided he couldn't go to the sanctuary covered in blood and scratches, so he drove to my mother's, who didn't live very far away. Upon sighting him she said, "My God, what happened to you?". Gary calmly replied that a koala had attacked him, Mum didn't believe him until he unwrapped the guilty party on the back seat. Gary was patched up and the koala got a home and treatment at the sanctuary.

Gary became quite a celebrity, and got his photo in the paper, wearing a tee shirt that said "Killer Koala", with a picture of a veracious looking koala on it; he also made a new friend that year. He had a soft spot for old people, he would spend lots of time talking and listening to them, they thought he was precious, as he was. This particular old lady, was very strange. She lived on a property in Mudgeeraba, surrounded by litterly hundreds of animals, dogs, by the dozens, cats, chooks, goats, you name it she had it.

Her house, if you could call it that was also full of animals, including the chooks and goats. The council had been on her back because of complaints from neighbours. She was too old and poor to care for them properly, some of them were in a sad condition, as she was herself. Gary took a liking to this eccentric lady and they formed a great friendship. She worshipped the ground he walked on, as he did as many jobs as he could to help her out.

One day he found a pony in a broken down chook house; it was locked in the house. He asked the lady (I have forgotten her name) if he could find a home for it. So one afternoon he arrived home with a rented horse float in tow, and we had a pony. It didn't take him long to find a home for it.

At his funeral I remember walking out of the funeral parlour through the hundreds of people that came, with my head lowered in grief, I noticed a pair of very large man's shoes on an old lady. It was his friend, although she hadn't left her house for a very long period, she came to the funeral, and was visibly distressed.

The last year of his life was the best for us, we were home again amongst family and friends, we both had good jobs, and the kids loved their new school and were doing well. We built a new home at West Burleigh on an acre of land. Life seemed perfect.

The day he died he woke me up at 5.45 a.m. all excited, he said there was a flock of white cockatoo on the back lawn, and I should come and have a look. I groaned and said "Go show the kids, they'll like them." I went back to sleep, I never spoke to him again, he left for work shortly after. The kids were watching telly that afternoon when the police arrived to tell me he had been involved in a fatal accident. This didn't sink in for a while, I just said, "What hospital is he in, I'll go straight away." They repeated the word fatal, still I couldn't comprehend. I still don't understand, even all these years later.

CHAPTER TWENTY ONE

My memories of my sister Carol
(Born in 1954)

CAROL IS THE YOUNGEST GIRL in the family, and to me always seemed so fragile that she would break if you squeezed her too tight. She became a strong and admirable woman whose strength I admire to this day.

When she was a kid, she was forever sticking things up her nose and one day when she was around three, her body was emanating a repugnant smell. As she went from one group of us to the other to play with, nobody wanted her near. Mum couldn't figure out what it was and eventually took her to the doctor and he pulled out a piece of foam rubber she had shoved up her nose three weeks earlier.

During Mum's childhood she learnt ballet, and after having seven girls, she was determined to have at least one of us become a prima ballerina. She was unsuccessful with the first six, and Carol was her last chance, so she bought a pair of second hand pink ballet shoes from the thrift store, three inches longer than Carol's feet, and every day after school, she would put Carol through a rigorous routine. Mum would stuff the toes of the shoes with cotton wool so Carol's feet would fill the cavities, and she would spin around with arms and legs flailing. I don't know which Carol thought was worse, ballet lessons or homework, but she eventually outgrew the shoes,

and as Mum couldn't afford another pair, the fun ended and her aspirations of becoming a ballerina came to an end. For Mum that is.

When Carol was around nine, she caused a real fuss in the household. A huge hole had been dug in the back yard and a septic tank lowered into it, but because the workers hadn't finished, they left the ladder down the hole and the lid slightly ajar. Carol and Shane were playing outside and she deliberately threw a ball down into the hole and told Shane to go and get it. He was only four at the time and was a little intimidated by Carol who was four years older, so he did what she said. As soon as he got to the bottom of the hole, she pulled the ladder out and closed the lid.

Not long after this, Mum noticed Shane was missing and organized a search party, and even after the police were called, and every neighbor went out looking, Carol didn't say anything. After three hours someone heard whimpering coming from the new septic tank, and on lifting the lid, there he was, crouched down on the ground. He was so worn out, all he could muster was, CCCAAARRROOOLLL, DDDIIIIIDDD, IIT. That night Mum sat Carol down and explained to her the danger in what she had done. Then she tanned the living daylights out of her, and sent her to bed. She never did anything like that again.

She was always trying to do things to get in Mum's good books, and not long after we moved to Bribie Island (where we had a real inside toilet), she decided to clean it and the hand basin while Mum was at the beach with Dawn. Not realizing that Mum diluted it before using it, she grabbed the bottle of phenol and as she had seen Mum do many time before, proceeded to wipe everything with it. We only lived a short distance from the beach, so Mum and Dawn were still dripping wet when they returned home. Both of them racing to get to the toilet before the other, Mum got there first, pulled her togs down, and sat on the toilet waiting for the relief that was to follow. She let Dawn in to pee before using the bath, however just as Dawn sat down, the burning on Mum's bum started.

The water still on their bodies from the beach, had a chemical reaction with the phenol, and by the time they realized what had happened, it was too late. Their backsides became raw with a red rash, and skin started peeling off. Needless to say, Carol got a good tongue lashing after that.

Carol was sexually molested by a family friend from the age of three, until she was in her teens, so life for her was very traumatic during her childhood. How does something like this happen with so many of us around? These types have a real talent for hiding such things from everyone, and instilled in their victims a fear I cannot imagine. Because Carol was the youngest girl he was able to manipulate her into believing that her whole family would be wiped out if she said anything. So he would take her for walks or to the shop and pretend they were an item.

When I think back to this time and reach into my deepest memories, I try to recall a period of time when I knew this was happening to her. I can't remember anything, and being only 7 at the time, I don't know what I would have done had I known. I know what I would do now, but back then for fear of the same thing happening to me, would I have just pretended it wasn't happening and thanked the Lord that it wasn't me.

Carol was very talented but I didn't realize just how talented she was, until later in life. She had a real knack with words, and wrote poetry so poignant you could envision what she had written. Her poems were echoes of experiences that touched her and those she loved, and her creative talents flowed in many of them. It made me realize that even after her traumatic childhood, she continued to experience things, both good and bad, that would shape her into the woman she is today.

Following are three of Carol's many poems, each of which are reflections of her past, and things she believed in.

Amelia
Amelia was an innocent,
her heart was void of pain.
Till her innocence was ravaged,
by men with sickened brains.
Amelia's all confused now,
the word has spread about.
Her world of hearts and flowers,
is turning inside out.
Her friends all seem to shun her,
though they say that nothing's changed.
But it's hard to miss the fact,
that they're somehow not the same.
And the men all whistle at her,
and some make snide remarks.
For Rape has reared its ugly head,
and left it's vivid mark.
So Amelia's all confused now,
the word has spread about.
And when Amelia slits her wrists.
the innocence runs out.

Footsteps
Who will tell the children,
if they're black or white.
Who will draw dividing lines,
between the day and night.
Running around the streets,
are little girls and boys.
The color of their feet,
makes no difference to their noise.
Who will tell the children,
what is good or bad.
Who will give them prejudices,
that their parents had.
Little children's footsteps,
pattering in the street.
How long before they care,
about the color of their feet.

Innocent
Of what good could I be to you?
What profit could I bring.
I'm innocent I swear it,
I've never done a thing.
Why are my brother's bleeding,
Why do their mother's cry.
Please tell me what's the reason,
for the hatred in your eyes.
I see you bearing clubs and knives,
too late, your aim I see.
A baby seal without defense,
your aim is meant for me.

Because Carol's body was abused for so long, and at such an early age, she experienced many drawbacks, including the inability to deliver her children naturally. For each of her three children, she had caesarians, and for many years after, she suffered with adhesions which are spider like webs that grow inside the body. When the pain is too great to bear, they are surgically removed. The problem is, they are caused by operations in the first place, so the more you're operated on over the years, the worse they become. This, on top of the cancer she is now fighting, has caused her to be in and out of hospitals most of her adult life. It was because of her early-uninvited sexual experiences, that she has suffered with many medical problems later in life.

When I saw her in December 2000, she was full of spirit and determined to beat this thing, and even though she was obviously still in a great deal of pain, the family gathering seemed to boost her mental attitude. She didn't want to close her eyes for fear of missing out on anything, and the reminiscing on the back verandah of her home for hours on end, kept her surprisingly alert, and close to her old self.

Being the center of attention is something Carol has always craved, but this time she yearned for it for a different reason. She was trying to draw in as many memories of our past as possible, and each one seemed to lift her spirit.

After spending some time with Carol and my three sons, I returned back to Canada, but after my return I could hear the life draining from her body with every call I placed. And even though we said our goodbyes at Christmas time, I desperately wanted to see her again, but didn't know if I would be strong enough. When it appeared that Carol needed full time home care, our sister Teresa took her long service leave early, and went down to Sydney to help Steve look after her. Whenever I called and Carol couldn't talk, Teresa would give me a blow by blow description of how she was, and what she was going through.

As time went by, the talks often turned to tears as Teresa's emotional strength gave way to grief at seeing the intense pain Carol was going through, and watching our sister's body fade away. As I was writing this memoir, every chapter was sent to Carol, and a little joke we had between the two of us was that she would keep it to herself until it was published. There were times however, when Teresa would read out loud to her, because she didn't have the strength to do it herself.

May 5th 2001, and another flight back to Australia, only this time I'm not alone. My husband, Keith and I received word that Carol was nearing the end of her journey. While at work on the Wednesday morning I had an overpowering urge to call Teresa to see how Carol was. The time difference between the two countries made it 11.30am in Vancouver, but only 4.30am in Sydney, so I was a little hesitant about calling as it was way too early to wake Teresa up.

As much as I tried to concentrate on work I couldn't, so I called Teresa and she picked the phone up immediately, as if she was waiting for my call. Carol asked to talk to me and

Teresa pressed the phone to her ear, but I didn't know what to say, and her words were slurred and at times unrecognizable. "Bloody Bob" she whispered, and as tears filled my eyes, I was angered, knowing that he was still on her mind and had control of her emotions even now.

To make her more comfortable, the nurses had given her another shot of morphine, so we could only talk for a short time, but I told her how much I loved her, and for her not to worry about any of us. I told her I wasn't going to say good-bye because we would see each other again, and I asked her to make me a promise. When she gets up there with Gary, there was to be no tripping of the dunny collector. We didn't want another mess to clean up when we got up there too. Teresa took the phone and walked outside and she started to cry. She was having a hard time watching Carol go, and she thought that it was strange that I had called when I did as she was thinking of calling me. As Carol's caregiver for the past 4 months, the palliative care hospital, had given Teresa a room so she could be near her.

Carol's husband Steve and the kids had gone home the night before for some rest, and it was just a coincidence that I had called. Teresa had just contacted them because Carol wasn't expected to last much longer. Hanging up was the hardest thing I have ever had to do, and as soon as I put the phone down, the floodgates opened and my emotions came pouring out. I half expected to be attending Carol's funeral when the plane touched down in Sydney, but when I called Teresa from the airport, she said that Carol was still hanging in. Keith and I caught a taxi to the hospital and with our luggage headed up to the third floor where Carol's room was.

Keith waited in the family room with the luggage, and as I entered Carol's room, my heart missed a beat. She had lost so much weight since the last time I saw her in December, I couldn't believe it was her. The nurses had just given her another morphine shot, so all I could do was hold her, and although she was just a shadow of herself, she was still as beautiful as ever. As Carol was sleeping, Steve arranged for accommodation at a motel nearby, and Keith and I checked in, got ourselves settled, and went back to the hospital later in the afternoon. By then Carol was awake, and although not able to greet us in her usual mirthful way, her smile and eyes acknowledged she recognized us.

Her waking hours were short as she was in a semi in-duced coma from all the drugs, and as she needed time with Steve and the kids, Donny, Mathew, and Melanie, we kept our visit short. Our motel was only a couple of blocks from the hospital, so we were handy. On the Friday morning around 8.30 we arrived at the hospital, took breakfast up to Teresa, and called in to see Carol. She had just been bathed and was sleeping so Keith and I decided to go into Sydney for a few hours. He was flying back to Vancouver the next day, and I was staying on for another week, so we decided to get out.

We took off, expecting to see Carol on our return, but as

we got out of the elevator and started walking towards her room, a nurse stopped me from entering. Carol had passed away at 10am that morning, just one hour after we left her. Although I was deeply sadden, I couldn't help but feel a sense of relief at knowing her struggle was over, and I felt more sorrow leading up to her death than after. I know this was because I had the opportunity to see her again just before she left us, and I could see that she was going to a better place.

Now I feel a sense of anger, not at her passing but rather her life. The first 15 years when she endured that dirty little mans body up against her. And to think, had he the chance to defend himself, I'm sure he would say she asked for it. That's right Bob, a three-year-old baby begged you to have sex with her, and you in return showed her where you would bury her mothers body if she told. Daddy dearest, how could you?

Carols funeral was a celebration of her life, with a collection of photo's and films flashed up on two large screens, every one reminding each and every one of us just how special she was. Fifteen hundred people attended her funeral, which goes to show just how many lives she affected during her short life. Our oldest sister Coral used to sing a song to Carol when she was small called "You Are My Special Angel", and wrote this poem from that song to read on the day of her funeral. Little did we realize at the time how true it was?

Our Angel

An Angel came down from Heaven above.

Sent down to Earth to show us love.

We all felt feelings we couldn't explain.

The Lord said I'm sorry, I need her again.

She has to come back to Heaven above.

So I can send her elsewhere, for someone to love.

So remember God said, this isn't goodbye.

You will see her again in the blink of an eye

We will all miss our Angel wherever we roam,

but we all must remember, she was only on loan.

CHAPTER TWENTY TWO

Carol's own memories of her childhood.

(Written after Christmas 2000, and again just before she passed away in May 2001)

I SUPPOSE IT'S ABOUT TIME I DID something about writing some of my childhood experiences down for your book. I have thoroughly enjoyed reading what you have sent to me so far so please keep it coming. I'm glad you gave everyone the opportunity to write something about their memories, but I hope you don't mind, but I think you should just keep it between us until it is published because it would give away too many of the surprises.

I've already told Teresa quite a few things about what happened to me in my childhood, but there is quite a bit of unhappy stuff that I would rather forget. I wasn't sure you wanted to hear all of it, but I'll go back in my memory as far as I can to bring it all to the forefront. I know we had lots of fun when we were growing up, when we would go down the beach and play, but there were also some very sad times and I find it difficult looking back that far.

I must admit some was brought back by the radiation treatment that I am having at the moment. During the treatment I have been strapped down and it just opens the floodgates as Bob used to do that to me when he wanted his way. I can remember it all starting when I was around three years old, but it could have been earlier for all I know. I never thought he could ever hurt me deliberately, but it was Bob, the father I loved so dearly.

I know he used to try with the older girls, but they never seemed scared like I was. They used to ask me if Dad ever did anything to me and of course I would deny it as I was just a little girl and he used to threaten to kill Mum or me and bury us in the bush, where no one would ever find us. I remember him taking me out and showing me a place he had in mind, and I'll tell you, it was very scary. He also used to tell me that no one would ever believe a little liar like me and that Mum would put me in a home away from everyone, and even though I could never imagine my Mum ever doing something so terrible to me, such things played on a little girls mind.

I remember on the odd occasion when I was getting more into my early teen years, around 12 or 13, that Dad would buy me things like jewelry and try and dress me up to look a little bit older, but I don't think it really fooled anyone. Our standard Saturday date as he used to call it, was a day at the trots and if he had a good day on the punt, then I'd get a gift. We were living on the Gold Coast Highway at the time, and Mum and Dad had split up a few months before. I stayed with him so I could look after Victor and Tony. All the other kids had basically left home and Shane was living on Chevron Island with Mum and her new boyfriend Barry. Oh, how I envied Shane, as Dad had a real knack of making you feel you were at fault for everything that went wrong with him.

I have often thought about confronting him, but to be honest I can't be bothered. He would be around 80 now, with one foot in the grave, and I have consolation in knowing that we will not end up in the same place, for he will rot in hell. That was the past and now I have to look to the future.

Teresa has been really helpful to me since I got sick again, and I don't know how I would have managed without her. I don't know when she sleeps but she is up all hours of the night and always seems to be there no matter what time it is, day or night when I wake up. She told me she would be here to help me in the end, but I feel bad because I take things out on her even though I don't mean to. The medication is making me sick and angry and I can't help feeling envious of her because she has her whole life to live and mine will soon be over.

I do feel I did the wrong thing by inviting Mum down for a couple of weeks at Christmas as Teresa was worked off her feet. I should have known better, but I put myself in Mum's shoes and was thinking that if it were my own daughter Melanie, I sure as hell would want to see her for myself how she was. I'll know better next time, as a matter of fact, I've already told Mum she won't be able to come back down and stay when I get better because I'll be spending all of my time looking after Steve and myself. She understands that I just won't have time or the patience for that matter to look after her as well especially now that she is in a wheelchair.

I'm getting tired and I must go, and I wish I could remember more about our childhood. There is one thing I would like to see one more time; All of my brothers and sisters together again holding hands, just like we did when we were kids. We had so much fun together. Through the bad times and good, we always had a smile on our faces and made each other laugh. I will write some more later when I'm feeling better.

Note: Carol passed away two months after writing this.

CHAPTER TWENTY THREE

My memories of my brother Victor
(Born in 1956)

ICTOR THE GREAT WAS THE string bean of the family and much taller than others his age, which gave you the notion that he was a lot older than he actually was. This, along with his good looks and blond hair, usually kept him out of trouble, even though he was usually the instigator. Victor was and still is a great source of information, but he was forever correcting his schoolteachers.

He went to great lengths to prove he was right in front of everyone, but one thing you should never do is correct a teacher in front of her pupils. One day, Mum got a visit from his religious teacher, Mrs. Carley declaring that she was unprepared for such a student, and because of his constant embarrassing outbursts, she was rethinking her choice of a teaching career.

Mrs Carley told Mum that she was so frustrated with his incessant talking, she threatened to tape his mouth shut, but after several warnings for him to keep quiet, he still continued, so she taped it shut with duct tape. In those days, parents didn't mind if their kid was punished this way, especially if it taught them a lesson.

Another day she told him that if he didn't stop disrupting her class, she would put a nappy on him. Well he stopped talking, but not for long, and she finally came to see Mum. She said she couldn't take it any longer, and couldn't stand the thought of having to face another day with him in it; she never went back to the school, but instead put a backpack on and left town.

Mum often had a fire going in the back yard to heat the water for washing, and our daily baths, and Victor and his younger brothers were always getting into trouble for playing with the flames. The fire seemed to draw them in and for sure every time she lit it, there they were, and she was always threatening to string them up if they went near it. Between this and the constant mud puddle they had in the back yard, they kept Mum on the go.

I feel bad about my lack of memory of my three youngest brothers, but because of our age differences, I have little memory of them when they were small. I was too busy with surfing and work, and hanging out with people in my own age group.

CHAPTER TWENTY FOUR

Victors memories of his childhood

MY FIRST FUNNY THOUGHTS OF growing up, or any for that matter, were of Gary who was 8 at the time, Carol 6, me 4 and Tony 3, going every Saturday afternoon down to the beach at Redcliffe or Scarborough. We would always sneak to the top of a small hill looking down about 20 meters to the back of some public toilets on the beach.

You see, every Saturday afternoon, a couple would be at the back of the toilets lying on a rug having sex. We never told anyone at all about our secret private display, and we always walked away from it just about falling over from laughing. Our last Saturday of ever seeing this couple again was when we decided to make it more interesting by actually participating in their display. The council rubbish bins (trash cans) around and on the beach in those days, was a 44 gallon drum and well, boys will be boys. Gary and I found the nearest rubbish bin, emptied the contents on the ground and rolled the large, heavy drum over to the top of our viewing platform on the top of our little hill.

When we saw the couple thrashing about like 2 WWF wrestlers and moaning out loud, we released the drum down the hill. Due to their minds and bodies being preoccupied, the couple didn't hear or see the drum hurtling down on them. We watched anxiously as the drum rolled all the way down the hill without losing direction and landed smack bang on the buttock of the male. We didn't wait around to witness the results of our participation and ran all the way home laughing so hard that we had tears running down our cheeks for hours afterwards. We went back to the little hill every Saturday for 3 more weeks, but unfortunately, never saw the couple again.

Good old Bribie Island (Woomera - Surf Side) and our huge house on the esplanade. God, from all of our Bribie frolics, where do I start? Mum used to wash our clothes in an old 44 gal (220 liter) drum set up in the back yard. The drum had a large square cut into it at the base so a fire could be lit in the bottom of it to heat a large copper tub full of water that was placed in the top of the open drum.

I remember Dad always saying to me to never touch the drum or the one inch plumbing pipe that ran through the middle of the drum from one side to the other. The copper tub would sit on the pipe above the raging fire below, and heat the water for the washing and our evening bath. One Saturday afternoon, Desley was babysitting Shane, Tony and I whilst Mum and Dad went to the local pub for the Saturday afternoon session and meat raffle. Desley was upstairs doing something whilst we boys were in the enormous back yard chasing the chickens and ducks around.

Tony needed to water the pony (pee) and decided to show Shane and I something he had discovered. We stood around the drum that was heating up the water in the copper tub and Tony started to pee on the side of the drum causing steam to rise and no pee run down the side to the ground. We thought this was amazing and told Tony to keep peeing, but to aim the stream into the 1 inch pluming pipe while we watched steam coming out the other end on the other side of the drum. What a surprise we all received when nothing came out the other side, not even on Tony's side.

We told Tony to keep peeing, which he did, and after 5 or 10 more seconds, Shane and I walked back around to Tony's side of the drum to see what was happening. Just as we arrived at his side, we saw a large gush of steam fly out of Tony's end of the pipe and hit him right in the groin. Well, it appeared that the other side of the pipe was blocked off inside, and when Tony urinated into the end of the pipe, it ran beyond the point of where the fire was below the pipe and built up pressure on the blocked side of the pipe.

When the pee had built up enough pressure due to becoming steam, it had to escape somewhere, and poor Tony of course who was still standing there with his penis hanging out of his shorts, bore the brunt of the pressurized steam. Shane and I couldn't stop laughing while Tony was running around screaming in pain. Desley heard the screaming in the back yard and looked out to see what had happened, and when she realized Tony needed medical aid, she grabbed the only thing Mum always grabbed when any of us were hurt, Mentholated Spirits (Metho) of course.

You see we always thought Mum got a kick out of watching us in excruciating pain after she applied Metho to any of our wounds. This in itself caused usually more intense pain than the injury or wound so as you can imagine, Tony wasn't about to let her catch him. Imagine Desley with a cotton ball full of Metho, chasing Tony around the yard, and finally catching him and applying Metho to his groin. Desley, Shane and I were in fits of laughter watching Tony jumping up and down after having Mentholated Spirits burn his groin area probably more than the steam ever did.

We used to have "cracker night" (Guy Faux night) on the Queen's birthday every year before which everyone would save for weeks and buy as many fireworks (crackers) as possible for the big night. In those days you could not only buy what we called the "big one" or " three penny bunger", but you could buy fireworks period. I recall the funniest (which was also the worst) cracker night ever. It was when I was around 10 years old (1966) and we lived across from the beach at Woorim on Bribie Island. Every Queen's Birthday holiday, we spent the afternoon digging foxholes and trenches on the beach, just like we read about and saw in the movies of WW1 battles.

We always had the best entrenchments on the island, and when we completed them, we would always leave at least one guard on each side of the battlefield to guard them against marauding parties wanting our battle zones. This particular year, Gary was in command of our side and I was his 2IC. Our team included Gary, Carol, Shane, Tony, Colin Jones (our next door neighbor) and me. Who cared who was on the other team, because we always won the battles. This was a particularly funny and violent year I thought. Funny, because of my memories of how much we laughed, and violent because of how many of us were hurt, and of the sadistic and brutal things we did. Now they seem brutal but when you're young, it just seems like fun.

I remember we were at home having an early dinner at around 4pm, and we were all anxious to get down to the beach prior to dusk around 5. This would allow us sufficient time to locate our foxholes, settle into them and scan the enemy lines for the ensuing battle to come. During the course of the battle, I remember every one of us told Tony not to have all of his crackers in one box, but to split them up into smaller boxes. This was in the event that if a spark fell into his box it wouldn't send his night up in smoke. Well there he was, on his hands and knees crawling between two foxholes in the trenches, but unbeknown to Tony, one of the enemy spotted his head or butt bobbing up and down as he was crawling, and threw a roll of Tom Thumbs right into his ammunition.

Tony had the largest amount of crackers on the beach that night and all of a sudden, all hell broke loose. I was in the foxhole next to where Tony was heading, Gary was in the foxhole behind Tony, and Shane was in the foxhole Tony had just retreated from. When we all saw the massive explosion of gunpowder and light and saw Tony jumping up and down on the spot trying to avoid the exploding crackers and skyrockets, we fell to the ground laughing so hard that we were all crying. When the laughter ceased quite some time later, and we collected ourselves, we stockpiled what ammunition we had left, and divided the crackers so as not to leave Tony out of the remainder of the battle.

Carol was dainty and threw like a girl, so we put her in the front line nearest the enemy. Gary and I were getting bored with the ease of the battle and decided to liven things up and crawled through our trenches to Carol's foxhole. When we approached Carol from behind, Gary grabbed her and I lit a cracker and threw it down the back of her pants. Well that was it for Carol because the cracker exploded of course, and burnt one of Carol's buttocks, and after receiving treatment from Mum she was taken to hospital.

The Joneses, had a Labrador dog and one day we grabbed it and tied a bunger to the end of it's tail and lit the fuse. We didn't expect the bunger to blow off the end of the dogs tail like it did but after that we never saw it again.

We moved from Bribie to the Gold Coast and lived at the Miami Caravan Park, and to earn some extra money, I used to help the Manager of the park on my school holidays.

Weekends and holidays were always busy with families on vacation and there was always an abundance of young girls. I had a tourist girlfriend who was staying at the park during the Christmas holidays and right next door to her was another girlfriend I had at the same time, and two caravans away I had another girlfriend. The caravan between my second and third girlfriend was old Holly Condon the loud mouth and trouble-maker.

After juggling my love life between these three girlfriends and my permanent girlfriend, what was about to happen, opened my eyes and made me more fearful of the wrath of a woman scorned. Old Holly Condon had finally caught on to me dating so many girls and had told them all one morning while I was cleaning out the ladies shower block in the caravan park. I recall turning around while I was cleaning and being faced with my worst fear, which was all three of my tourist girlfriends confronting me at once. Their demand of me was that I had to make up my mind about which one of them I wanted as my girlfriend over the next 24 hours.

We were to all meet at the ladies shower block the next morning to hear my decision. I still don't know whether to curse old Holly Condon for what she did to me, or pat her on the back. During the next 24 hours, I was offered and had sex with all three girls many times over. You see each one thought that sex was the only thing on my mind. All three thought they could persuade me to choose them and was willing to give me sex either because it was what I wanted, or just to stop the other girl from having me probably out of bitchiness.

What a surprise they all received when I didn't show up the next morning. There they were all standing outside of the ladies shower where we had planned to meet, as I drove past heading down to the beach, with my permanent girlfriend in the drivers seat.

CHAPTER TWENTY FIVE

My memories of my brother Tony
(Born in 1957)

THE SECOND YOUNGEST, TONY WAS a healthy active boy until he turned 11, at which time he developed Rheumatoid Arthritis, and although he's been in constant pain ever since, he has a strong will and always strived to improve.

I remember when he was young, Mum would have to strap braces on his arms and legs when he went to bed, and if he didn't wear them his body would curl up into a little ball, and she would have to un-peel him like a banana before he could stand up. This process took a good hour, but when he got older he became the typical rebellious teenager and refused to wear them any longer; with or without the braces he was in constant pain.

Everything Tony did was laborious and painful, and I can remember him heading off to school with his school bag, with only a few items in it, still weighing him down. He would make regular trips to the hospital for gold injections and we always joked about how much he was worth.

I truly can't remember ever seeing Tony, Shane and Victor apart when they were growing up. They were all a year apart in age and did everything together and they were like the three stooges, always dobbing on each other, but the best of buddies who stuck together like glue. Forever playing games on the Bribie sand dunes, with towels wrapped around their heads like turbans, or tied under their chins like Superman, they would jump off the highest sand dune and soar.

Tony loved playing in the mud with Shane and Victor and even if it hadn't rained for weeks there was always a puddle in the back yard where they drove their pretend army ducks and blew each other to smithereens. Mum was forever tanning their hides and sending them to their room for dirtying yet another set of clothes. They also enjoyed fishing together and all three would fashion fishing lines out of string and a twig and tie bread from the end in hopes of catching something for Mum.

My memories of Tony growing up are few because by the time he and his younger brother came along I had other interests and was starting to notice the opposite sex, and the one thing I definitely didn't want around was an annoying younger brother.

CHAPTER TWENTY SIX

Tony's memories of his childhood

I DON'T REMEMBER TOO MUCH about Redcliffe because I was only four or five, but something that always stuck in my mind, is when I almost fell over Cleo (the dog) at the back door after he overdosed on sleeping pills. He almost died but Mum fixed him and he got better pretty soon after that.

I also remember going to the swimming pool at Redcliffe and one day we spied on a couple going at it behind the toilet block. We thought we should try and disrupt them so one of us turned the tap on so we could flood them out, but they didn't even slow down. Behind the toilet block was a hill so we rolled a drum down on them but I don't know what happened after that because we all ran off.

When we lived in Thornton Street in Surfers Paradise Gary

used to go out early in the morning and take the milk money that people had left out for the milkman. He showed Victor what to do to get all the spending money he needed and Victor showed Shane and me, but if we were late and the milk man had already been, we would drink some of the milk instead.

I decided I didn't want to do it any more and told Victor and Shane that they're going to get caught if they keep it up. The next thing, there's a policeman at the door and Victor's telling him that the whole thing was my idea. I just laid in bed, terrified that they were going to take me away. Instead, every time Mum cried over the next couple of days, we would cop a flogging with the electrical cord or egg lifter from the BBQ. It wasn't long after that we moved to Western Australia.

The move to Western Australia was a great trip that took us a week to drive over across the Nullabore Plains. We slept by the roadside each night, and while crossing we would come across aborigines with spears and boomerangs. Before crossing the Nullabore, we spent a short time in a little town called Eucla, where Gary went down to this old dry concrete water tank at the bottom of this hill, and in it he found some snakes and spiders, which he killed and threw away.

Not long after that, three dinky di abo's came along dressed in lap lap's and carrying spears and nulla nulla's, and in broken English, they asked Gary what happened to the snakes that they stored in the old dry tank. Apparently they had stored them in there until they were finished hunting, but Gary said he didn't know anything about them and they went on their way.

I remember when I was small, I had an accident one day when I decided to pee into a pipe in a copper boiler Mum used to boil water in for our bath. It must have been blocked or something because it shot back out of the pipe straight on my poor little willie and I screamed in agony. I can't remember which of my older sisters done it, but they rubbed some stuff on it to make it better, but boy it hurt.

Even though I was near top of my class in every class, (grades 2,3,4) school days on Bribie were not that exciting, and I soon went down hill. There was this girl name Jill who was the ugliest girl in school and was teased by everyone. As soon as the bell sounded to go back to class after little lunch and big lunch, someone would yell out "last one back loves Jill". Boy what a scramble that was.

There were a few wild donkeys and horses roaming around the island, and one day we decided to try to horseback and pat one of them. Shane was lying just in front of it on the ground and someone slapped it on the rump and it took off straight over the top of him, kicking him in the head. It was pretty funny at the time, and would also explain a few things.

Victor, Shane and I would have to go to Sunday school each week, but we didn't mind being Catholics and religious. I remember being in school when I was about eight, and we would catch horse flies, and stick a small piece of straw up their you know where. With a piece of cotton tied to it, it could only fly where we wanted it. Looking back on life on Bribie compared to now, it seemed like such an adventure.

CHAPTER TWENTY SEVEN

My memories of my brother Shane
(Born in 1958)

SHANE IS THE YOUNGEST, AND WHEN I think of him as a toddler, I'm reminded of one of those little pit bull-mastiff terriers, or as an Aussie would put it " build like a brick shithouse" He was the spitting image of his older brother Gary when he was little and I remember him as a little ball of fun that turned into the eternal optimist of the family. One day when we were all down the beach, Shane came up to Mum with a hand full of beach towels, that he thought had been abandoned. He didn't realize at the time that the owners had simply left them on the beach while they had gone for a swim.

A favourite activity handed down from the older siblings

in the family was to bury some poor soul up to their neck in sand and wait for the tide to come in. This was at times quite scarey for the recipient because you never knew if they were going to come back to your rescue before it was too late. It usually started out with a group of us playing on the beach, with everyone making a cumulative effort in getting along. This soon became boring however, and in order to liven up the day, someone would suggest a burial.

Well, maybe not in those words, but believe me, this is what it felt like for the person who was just about to be sacrificed; and somehow everyone knew about it except the sacrificial lamb. What started out as an understanding by everyone that they were simply trying to dig the "deepest hole" or "tallest sand castle" or the start of another one of our famous trenches, usually ended up a practical joke for some unsuspecting soul. Of course, we always came back to the rescue, but by this time one of us was sure to endure the wrath of the poor bastard we were digging out.

Mum could always tell when Shane, Tony and Victor were up to no good because they constantly gave themselves away by sneaking around the house and whispering to each other. She would ask, "What are you little buggers up to?" Of course they would deny everything until one of them gave in and blamed the other two.

I recall one day when they wanted to buy lollies, and didn't have any pocket money. Even if they did chores around the house, Mum couldn't afford to give them pocket money, so they snuck behind the local shop and stole a few empty soft drink bottles to cash in. They even had the nerve to run around the block so the shop keeper could see them coming from the other direction, and cash the bottles in at the same store they stole them from. This went on for quite some time until Shane dropped one of the bottles as they were running off with them, and Mr. Walner heard the noise. He comes running to the back of the store and sees the three of them scrambling over the fence. To make restitution they had to work in Mr Walner's shop for a week, but I'm sure he paid for it again in some way, even if he didn't realize it.

CHAPTER TWENTY EIGHT

Shane's memories of his childhood.

I HAVE REALLY GOOD MEMORIES OF Bribie Island, like always going for long walks along the beach or through the bush. Being only 7, 6, and 5, Victor, Tony and I being the last 3 of 13 we got away with a lot and did anything we wanted to do. Cracker nights were always great fun, and we would go over to the beach and dig trenches and fox holes all day so we could have a war when it got dark.

We spent a lot of time in and around the old concrete buildings (gun emplacements), left on the beach after the war. They were on the beach about 50 meters from our house and they were pretty high in some areas, from the surf that had washed the sand away from the foundations. In some parts the drop was only a couple of feet, but in others it was up to 15 and higher. One day I was pushed off and landed on my back, which nearly broke, and I spent a lot of time recovering.

Not far from our house was the News Agent and General Store, and one of our mate's father was the owner. He gave his son and one of us a job of cutting the tops off the front page of the newspapers so he could get a refund for the ones he hadn't sold. Every time he left us sitting on the floor behind the counter we would grab a packet of smokes, and each time we took a packet, we would smoke three of them, and bury the rest of them in the building on the beach. This went on for some time until one day when Desley and one of my mate's older brothers got suspicious, and they followed us. We had buried 64 packets of cigarettes but because they were all opened, they couldn't be sold at the shop, so they were sold at a party and the money that was collected, went to the shop owner.

A lot of time was spent swimming, and playing war games in the bushes between the house and the beach, and we were always finding things like sea snakes and baby sharks, that had been trapped by the low tides in water holes along the beach. We would take them home and put them in the bathtub, and Mum would have a fit whenever she found them. Way up the beach was the fishermens cabins, which we used to break into and eat their powdered milk and whatever else we could find. Then there was our other mate, whose father owned the local hotel, but alcohol wasn't real big with us until years later.

Then there was the time when we found a sugar bag full of Caustic Soda, that Mum used to use to clean the downstairs toilets, but to us it looked a lot like sugar. Being as young as we were, we decided to sample some of it and our mouths were covered in blisters for ages. Most of the time we were good kids involved in petty crime like stealing empty soft drink bottles from shops.

The first time Nippers (cadet life savers) started in Australia was when we lived on Bribie Island, so Victor, Tony and me signed up, and every week end we would all go down the beach to learn how to do lifesaving and surfing. Back then girls weren't allowed in the club but they are now.

When we moved to Surfers Paradise we were enrolled at St Vincent's Catholic School and although the nuns tried, our ways didn't change that much. Victor and Tony were alter boys and they used to drink the wine and eat the bread on the Vestry at the back of the church. One weekend all three of us broke into the priest's house and laid on his bed, ate his chips, and drank his coke while watching his TV. By the time we noticed that he had returned home it was almost too late and we nearly got caught. While he was coming in the front door, we were running out the back. Boy was it a close call.

On most weekends, we would hang around Surfers Paradise looking for ways to get a quick buck. There was this Pepsi machine, which was up in the Chevron Hotel parking lot, and we would get our drinks from it for nothing and take them to the movies.

Once, when living in Surfers, the three of us wagged school for a whole two weeks without anyone knowing, except Carol, and the only reason they caught us was because the school bus drove past us with the entire class on board. We were made to stay after school till we passed all of our exams, and it wasn't long after that we left the Catholic School and started going to the State School, which we hated. Victor, Tony and me did everything together and one day we broke into the classroom at our new school and just about destroyed it.

When I think back to our younger days, we got away with murder, and if Mum only knew half of what we did she would have skinned us alive.

CHAPTER TWENTY NINE

Oh How Time Flies

ECAUSE OF OUR AGE DIFFERENCES, my memories of my older and younger siblings are few and far between, however those around my age are uncluttered. I wish I had the foresight to see how easy one forgets, and if I had, I would have harnessed as much as I could as we were growing up together.

So much has happened after we all moved away from home and the following is a summary of where everyone is now. Starting with Mum, and although some of us are worlds apart, we are still as close as ever.

- Mum continued to be an important part of our lives even after we all moved away from home and had our own families. She has for most of her life lived within a short distance from most of us and whenever we could, we celebrated special occasions with her.

  At 84 she now lives in a Government run semi-retirement home in Cleveland. It is a self contained unit, and quite comfortable, with its own small garage in which she parks her battery operated motorized chair. Every morning, she takes it out for a leisurely drive to the local shop where she buys the morning paper. She parks it outside of the shop and beeps the horn until she attracts their attention and they wait on her hand and foot.

  After 9 3/4 years of pregnancies and raising 13 children, Mum is content to sit back and watch the world go by. The only regret she has in her life is one she would not wish on anyone. A parents nightmare of watching four of her children pass away and wishing each time that it was her instead.

- Coral now 65 and her husband Barney are retired and currently touring Australia in their camper van. They plan on seeing as much of the country as they can before settling down in their new home in beautiful north Queensland. They have four children; the oldest Teresa, followed by Jamin, Gavin and Nicole.

- Dawn now 61 and her husband Laurie live in the Sydney suburb of Busby. Dawn worked most of her life for the Education Board of New South Wales, however her and Laurie who have three children, Pat, Steve and Dianne are now retired. A few times a year Dawn travels up to Cleveland and spends time with Mum.

- Had Jacqueline survived she would now be 59 and no doubt an admirable woman. I feel sorry for her loss: for what she missed out on from not knowing the rest of her family, and the affect she would have had on us, had she not passed away at such an early age.

- Billy would have continued being a successful bricklayer, and had his path been unbroken, at 58 he would be planning his early retirement, and enjoying the treasures harnessed by the successful business he had before his accident. He and his wife Wendy had two children, Rebecca and David.

- Teresa, 57, lives on the Gold Coast with her husband Arthur and their two surviving sons John and Darryl. Shawn passed away in 1983 and would be 29 today. Once a month Teresa travels to Cleveland, about 60 kilometers from the Gold Coast to spend the week end with Mum.

- Barton now 56 lives in the Western Australia suburb of Bibra Lake with his wife Maxine and son Justin. He drives semi trailers for a living and has two daughters Kimiko and Lealani from a previous marriage. Bart is still active and rides his big Mal surf board every day.

- Myself. On a recent visit back to Australia I took a day trip to where my fondest memories come, Bribie Island. Although it has changed, and the population has grown from a small village to that of a large tourist destination, some of the things that were familiar to me 38 years ago were still there, and brought back many memories. Although remodeled and now used as a vacation home, the house we once lived in still stands opposite the beach and sand dunes we all played on as children. After many years and several generations of children playing on them, the gun emplacements across the road on the beach had to be demolished because of corrosion and instability. The local Bribie Pub stands as a testament to the good old days, and across the street, the old fig tree remains firmly planted against the wind of time. It's leaves protecting the locals waiting for the bus as it did for us when we were kids. It seems like only yesterday when I stood under that same tree waiting for the school bus with all of my friends; but oh how time flies!.

    I was a homebody for most of my own children's school years, and when I finally went back to work full time in 1988 I was fortunate enough to work for a company on the Gold Coast that believed in nurturing and training its employees. My boss was a gentleman who believed that lack of education did not necessarily mean lack of ability, and my low self esteem was soon allayed by the many educational workshops I attended during the 4 years I work at Morris International. This was a turning point in my life, and I believe I would not be where I am today if it wasn't for the opportunity and training that Mr Morris invested in me throughout my time with his company.

When I moved to Canada in 1992, I started working for a company jointly owned by Mr Morris and a Canadian gentleman, and as luck would have it, Jim Ripplinger also had the same work ethics and values as Terry Morris and for that I will always be grateful. I am now CEO of this company and in fact, it was because of Jim and Terry that I met my husband Keith. He came to Australia from Canada on an exchange program between their two companies, and he worked at Morris International for 12 months back in 1991; as soon as he walked in the door, it was love at first sight.

Much has happened since I left home as an 18 year old, and at 54, I now live and work in British Columbia, Canada with my husband of 11 years Keith, and I have gone back to school to further my education in Business Management. I have experienced many things since leaving home, including a 22 year marriage to my first husband Carl, and three amazing sons, Jason, Jeffrey and Wade.

- Desley, 53 lives not far from Mum and along with her husband Mick, is Mum's care giver. Every day she cooks Mum's supper and drops around for a few minutes to chat and see how she is. Mick and Desley have been married now for 4 years. Desley has 4 children from her first marriage; Alan, Leeanne, Adam and William.

- Gary was a bricklayer by trade however he would not be content to rest on his laurels, and at 52 would have been actively involved with the children in his community just as much as he was before he passed away. He and his wife Gay had two children Rebecca and Correy.

- Carol would have continued writing beautiful poetry, and doting on her new grandchild born just after she passed away. She was a strong woman and has left a legacy of love with everyone she knew. Carol and her husband Steve had three children, Donny, Mathew and Melonie.

- Victor 48 lives with his wife Rose in the Sydney suburb of Mount Prichard. He works for the Australia Railroads and is currently going for a degree in Psychology. Victor has three sons, Victor, David and Timothy, from a previous marriage.

- Tony, now 47 lives in the beautiful New South Wales coastal town of Lennon Heads. He maintains the grounds of the unit that he shares with his younger brother Shane.

- Shane who also lives in Lennon Heads, is a bricklayer by trade, and at 46 is enjoying the freedom and laid back surroundings the small coastal town has to offer.

CHAPTER THIRTY

Conclusion

I TRULY BELIEVE THAT WE MAKE the decision on how the good and bad things we experience throughout our lives, affect us as we grow older. Whether we simply stand by and watch, or actually take part, we have a choice to learn from or ignore them, and I feel the negative things are just as important as those that make us happy.

Without these experiences and feelings, would we know how to respond to something as an impulse

- *If we don't experience pain and sorrow, are we able to comfort those that do?*

- *If we don't have laughter and joy in our lives are we able to openly recognize these qualities in someone else?*

- *Does the experience of being comforted by someone, only to have him or her turn on you, teach you to recognize the demon concealed behind a mask?*

Experience teaches you to recognize a mistake when you make it again. If the path you took the first time wasn't the right one, then take another this time, and see where it takes you. It's your choice, and it's never too late to make a bad turn into the right direction.

Choices I made in my past were right for me at the time,

and if I had my life to live over again, there is little I would change. Good or bad, all of our adventures are what shapes us into the people we are today.

As I leaf back through our memories, it becomes apparent that they were stronger for those who have passed than those remaining, and I am reminded of someone being recognized for their achievements only after they are gone and not here to enjoy the accolades.

Don't wait until it's too late to let them know how much you care.

CHAPTER THIRTY ONE

Glossary

A Real Dill = Idiot.
Abo's = Aborigines.
Ambulance bay = Similar to a Fire or Ambulance hall.
Army Duck = Amphibian, land and sea vehicle
Arsehole = Arrogant son of a bitch.
Arsy = Lucky.
Barbie = Barbeque.
Bastard = Arsehole.
Big Lunch = Lunch recess.
Bolted = Took off.
Boot = Trunk.
Bouncer-Net = Babies low bouncing bed made of net.
Brickie = Short for bricklayer.
Brollie = Umbrella.
Browns Cows = Standing around like cows, not doing anything.
Bubble and Squeak = Left over mashed potato, pumpkin and other vegetables, grilled on the stove and usually served with Breakfast. Similar to Hash browns only better :)
Buggers = little devils, or mischief-makers.
Bungers = Fire crackers.
Carbuncle = A sore similar to a boil.
Carpet Snake. A large Non Venomous snake in Australia.
Chinwaged = Talked or reminisced.
Chipped in = Give a hand, helping out.
Chooks = Chickens.
Chunder = another way of saying Vomit.
Ciggies = Cigarettes.
Cocker Spaniel = Type of dog.

Consonance = Harmony, peace.
Copped = Got a lot of ribbing or name calling.
Copper = Large 40 gallon drum used to boil water. Also refers to a police man.
Cracker Night = Fireworks.
Cuppa = A cup of tea.
Cutie = good looking, cute.
Dead set = really, fair dinkum, honestly, riggy didge.
Dill = An idiot or fool.
Dingo = Wild dog.
Dings = Dints or holes caused by wipe out.
Dinky Di = Fair Dinkum, honestly
Dob = To tell on. I.e. I didn't do it, Wendy did.
Drongo = a real idiot.
Dripping = Lard.
Dunny = Toilet.
Farmlet = Small farm.
Farted = Passed wind.
Fortnightly = Every two weeks
Getting his jollies off = Masturbating.
Godsend = Welcomed
Going at it = Hard at it, or doing the best you can. Usually referring to sex.
Grog = Booze or Beer.
Gun-in-Placement = during the war, large cement structures were placed along the beach to house huge guns and ammunition.
Hard Up = Poor.
Hard Yakka = Hard Work.
Hell to Pay = in trouble.
High School or Big School = Secondary School.
Hop Skip and Jump = Short distance.
I'm outa here = Out of here.
In and Out word = F**k.

Innens = The inside (gut) of a chicken.
Jetty = Pier.
Let one drop = Farted.
Little Lunch = Morning recess.
Little School = Primary School
Lollies = Candy.
Mince = Ground beef
Mob = A large group of people.
Nappy= Diaper.
Nippers = Cadet Life Savers. "Little kids who nip at your ankles "
Nulla Nulla's = A throwing stick that helps the spear go further and faster.
Nursed = to hold or cradle a baby. Since coming to Canada I've learnt that you can't nurse someone else child without getting into trouble. To Nurse something in Australia doesn't mean the same as Canada, which is to breast-feed.
OK Bar = Similar to an Oh Henry bar.
Our lot = All of our family.
Out House = Outside dunny.
Patrol Cap = A cap worn by life savers during surf carnivals. Each surf club in Australia has it's own cap to distinguish one competitor from the other; If your cap comes off during a competition, you are disqualified.
Peeping tom = Pervert.
Pension and Child Endowment = Government assistance.
Pissed = Annoyed. Also means drunk as a skunk
Pissed Off = Annoyed.
played house = make believe or pretend.
Pulling her leg = Exaggerating.
Pullets = Small chickens.
Punt = Make a bet.
Put the Kettle on = Boil water and make a pot of tea.
Quid = A dollar.

Ribbed = Tease or annoy someone.

Rip = A strong current that can pull you out to sea.

Rissoles = Mince with chopped up tomatoes, onions, celery and sweet pickles, rolled into balls and coated in egg and breadcrumbs and fried in dripping. Also known as meatballs.

Rubbers = Erasers.

Ruckus = Noise.

Sacked = Fired from his job.

Safari Suit = Suit similar to an African Hunter suite.

Sin bin = into trouble, grounded, sent to the corner for misbehaving.

Skite = Brag.

Sloppy Joe = Pullover or sweat shirt.

Sure Fired = Guaranteed.

Sure thing = Guaranteed.

Tanned the living daylights out of = A severe beating or form or punishment.

Tanning their hides = Belting on the bare skin.

Technicolor Yawn = Vomit.

Telegram Boy = Delivered telegrams.

The Beatles = A popular singing group in the sixties.

Togs = Swim suite.

Tongue Lashing = To reprimand, or a good talking to.

Toungy = French kiss.

Trots = Harness racing. Horse race using a carriage. Also a term used to describe the runs or gastric.

Tyre = Rubber covering for a car wheel.

Vegies = Vegetables.

Wagged = Skipped without permission.

Whinge = Sulking, moody.

Willies = Pee.

Water the pony = Pee.

W.W.2 = World War Two.

2IC = 2ND in charge

Yabbies = Small fresh water type of crayfish.

ISBN 141203893-6

9 781412 038935